A LAMP FOR MY FEET

# A Lamp for My Feet

Elisabeth Elliot

VINE
BOOKS

Servant Publications
Ann Arbor, Michigan

Vine Books is an imprint of Servant Publications designed
to serve Evangelical Christians.

Published by Servant Books
P. O. Box 8617,
Ann Arbor, Michigan 48107

Cover illustration © 1985 David Hile
Book design by John B. Leidy

Printed in the United States of America
ISBN 0-89283-352-1

5 6 7 8 9 10     95 94 93 92 91

*Thy Word is a lamp to guide my feet
and a light on my path.*
*—Ps 119:105*

# Introduction

THERE IS NOT MUCH OCCASION in America today to walk dark pathways with only a little lamp. It is a world filled with artificial light of many kinds—streetlights, traffic lights, headlights, floodlights, neon lights, flashlights, klieg lights, spotlights. But for all of man's history, until this century, lamps were needed. In ancient times a tiny clay lamp was sometimes fastened to the thong of a sandal, so that the pool of light cast was sufficient only for a single step. The traveler took that step and found light enough for the next. So the psalmist wrote, "Thy word is a lamp to guide my feet and a light on my path" (Ps 119:105 NEB). Solomon exhorted his son to observe his father's commands and not to reject his mother's teaching, "for a command is a lamp, and teaching a light" (Prv 6:23 NEB).

Approaching the age of sixty, I think it is reasonable to admit that I am, by the biblical norm for life expectancy, old. In America today it is forbidden to use the word. We are senior citizens, golden agers, keen-agers, mature, anything but old. The assumption is that old equals useless. It has not always been so. In other times and places old has been a term of respect, because the old were assumed to have learned one or two things which could help to make the pathway of life a little clearer to those who followed. It was not thought that the old had learned all they could hope to learn, however. To me, old age is a gift. It is therefore a privilege. It is therefore a responsibility. I have a great deal yet to learn. I am sure of that, and by the grace of God I want to learn it. May I say with the psalmist, "I have thought much about the course of my life and always turned back to thy instruction." And, "I have found more joy along the path of thy instruction than in any kind of wealth" (Ps 119:59, 14 NEB).

9

To me, the commandments, that is, all that the word of God comprises, are a lamp. This book is made up only of reflections—reflections of the true light (though the reflector may distort), written over a period of five or six years, indoors, outdoors, usually early in the morning in some solitary place, but occasionally in an airplane or motel room. I have always been aware, ever since I was very small, of needing direction. I have gotten it—first from parents who were quite clear about what was right and what was wrong, what they wanted of us and what they didn't want. I got it from teachers in public school (they were allowed in those unenlightened days to make what are now called "value judgments") and from teachers in Sunday school. I got it from the Bible and from many books. Before I learned to read, I was read to—at least twice a day from the Bible and usually from another book or two as well. At family prayers my father sometimes read a children's paraphrase of the Bible, but when he opened his own Bible it was the Authorized Version (King James). We heard it seven days a week, and consequently our minds were filled with thousands of phrases (effortlessly memorized) of flawless English and shaped by those majestic cadences. This was a priceless gift from our parents, which of course we had no appreciation for at the time. Growing up, I began to be aware of something far more important: my parents really believed that Book and honestly tried to live their whole lives in the light that it shed.

As soon as I learned to read, I was given a leather-bound Bible, inscribed by my parents, which I kept on my bedside table and carried to church. Occasionally I read it by myself, but not very much, so far as I remember, until I went away to boarding school. Homesickness drove me to seek comfort where I knew my parents had found it—in the Bible. My father had given me Deuteronomy 31:8 (AV) to lean on: "The Lord, He it is that doth go before thee; he will be with thee, he will not fail thee, neither forsake thee: fear not, neither be dismayed." Strong words for a fourteen-year-old, words originally spoken by Moses when he turned over to Joshua the staggering burden of leading Israel. It did not occur to me to question my right to claim them. It seemed reasonable to believe that the God who would lead Joshua and had promised not to fail or forsake him would most certainly not fail or forsake a lonely girl. If there was nothing for Joshua to fear in the face of a so much greater task, there was nothing for me to fear either. I confess I was still afraid, sometimes, and have been afraid since those school years. Far more often I have been dismayed, but the lamp has always been there, shining its light if only I would pay attention and walk where it shone, reminding me that there is, after all, no real reason for fear.

Many students ask me for help and direction for their lives. It is always heartening to know that there are those who are willing to receive the kind they know I want to offer, for I always go back to my source: "the path of Thy commandments," and I desperately want them to find what I have found along that path: joy. So often they fear it will be something quite other than joy. "But look," I say, "if we're confused, we need somebody to show us the way and tell us what to do—in other words, we need a Master. He has been this way before. Wouldn't a sensible person pay attention to what He says and conscientiously try to understand, to apply the truth, and obey the instructions? He's leading us to the promised land! There will be fullness of joy there, and there is plenty of joy en route. Believe me." So I offer these suggestions which have helped me for more than half a century:

*Read the Bible.* Buy one if you haven't got one, because you need a copy you can mark. Today there are many excellent modern translations, for example, the New English, the New International, The Living Bible, and J.B.Phillips' translation of the New Testament. Reading the Bible takes time, but it is worth more than gold. Figure out how much time you spend daily on things that are worth nothing, then decide how much you can give to Bible reading. My father used to point out that no matter how thick a book may be, it can be got through if you spend fifteen minutes a day at it.

*Pray*—before, during, and after your reading. Ask God to help you to understand and obey. Let the words of Scripture shape your prayers. (I do not mean to suggest here that prayer books should not also be used. They are full of prayers shaped by Scripture, prayers which have stood the test of time, but it is good to learn to pray while we are reading.)

*Meditate.* Learn to be silent. God has told us to be still and know that He is God. Think of that fact in the context of the passage you have read. Give the Holy Spirit a chance to enlighten you. Our prayer should be, "Speak, Lord, for Thy servant heareth," not "Hear, Lord, for Thy servant speaketh."

*Apply the truth.* We need the Lord's help here especially, to show us what these words mean in terms of our own obedience. Pray: "Whatever You show me, Lord, by your grace I'll do it."

*Obey.* Now. Today. Do the thing required. If you see nothing that is required, remember the most important thing that is always required: trust God. Don't be afraid.

This is a simple book, the fruit of some of my quiet times. As I have reread it, I find that certain themes recur, lessons I have been working on all my life: trust, obedience, the sovereignty of God, sacrifice, suffering, strength, succor, consolation, mystery, and paradox. The recurrence of certain passages, certain applications of the Word, is evidence of how slow a learner I am and how often my Teacher needs to assign a review. If the tone sounds didactic, it is primarily because I have tried to take down the lesson as it applied to *me*, without argument, without equivocation, without pulling punches.

I do not mean to pontificate. You may find quite a different lesson in a passage I have cited. Let the Spirit of God teach you. I do not mean the book to be read at a single sitting, and I most emphatically do not mean it to be read *in place of* Bible and meditation. It is only meant to be a help. If you have only five minutes, don't read my book, read God's. It will be a lamp for your feet.

Magnolia, Massachusetts
February 1985

# 1 Why Bother to Pray?

IF GOD IS SOVEREIGN, and things will be as they are going to be anyway, why bother to pray? There are several reasons. The first is really all we *need* to know: God has told us to pray. It is a commandment, and if we love Him we obey his commands.

Second, Jesus prayed. People sometimes say that the only reason for prayer is that *we* need to be changed. Certainly we do, but that is not the only reason to pray. Jesus was not being made more holy by prayer. He was communing with his Father. He was asking for things. He thanked God. In his Gethsemane prayer He was beseeching the Father to prevent what was about to take place. He was also laying down his own will.

Third, prayer is a law of the universe. As God ordained that certain physical laws should govern the operation of this universe, so He has ordained the spiritual law. Books simply will not stay put on the table without the operation of gravity—although God could cause them, by divine fiat, to stay. Certain things simply will not happen without the operation of prayer, although God could cause them, by divine fiat, to happen.

The Bible is full of examples of people doing what they could do and asking God to do what they couldn't do. In other words, the pattern given to us is both to work *and* pray. Nehemiah and the people of Israel worked hard to build the wall of Jerusalem but were strenuously opposed by Sanballat and Tobiah, who banded together with Arabs, Ammonites, and Ashdodites to attack. "So we prayed to our God," wrote Nehemiah, "and posted a guard day and night against them" (Neh 4:9 NEB). □

## 2 Refreshment

"HE WHO REFRESHES OTHERS will himself be refreshed" (Prv 11:25).

"If you . . . satisfy the needs of the wretched . . . the Lord will satisfy your needs" (Is 58:10, 11 NEB).

Do you often feel like parched ground, unable to produce anything worthwhile? I do. When I am in need of refreshment, it isn't easy to think of the needs of others. But I have found that if, instead of praying for my own comfort and satisfaction, I ask the Lord to enable me to give to others, an amazing thing often happens—I find my own needs wonderfully met. Refreshment comes in ways I would never have thought of, both for others, and then, incidentally, for myself.

Lord, be as the dew to me today, as You were to Israel, that I may "flower like the lily" (Hos 14:5 NEB). □

## 3 My Own Fault

SOMEONE WHO IS SUFFERING as a result of his own foolishness or failure may read these words. These griefs are hard indeed to bear, for we feel we might easily have avoided them. We have no one to blame but ourselves, and there isn't much consolation *there*. Sometimes we imagine that we must bear this kind of trouble alone, but that is a mistake. The Lamb of God, slain for us, has borne all of our griefs and carried all of our sorrows, no matter what their origin. All grief and sorrow is the result of sin somewhere along the line, but Christ received them willingly. It is nothing but pride that keeps me from asking Him to help me to bear the troubles which are my own fault.

Lamb of God, who takes away the sin of the world, take away mine.

I take Him at His word indeed,
Christ died for sinners—this I read—
And in my heart I find a need
Of Him to be my Savior.

> (Dora Greenwell) □

## 4 One Reason for Darkness

MANY GREAT SAINTS have experienced what they could only describe as the absence of God, when their souls have entered into a dark night. Abraham was overcome by a horror of great darkness. No doubt this is one of the necessary lessons for some who share most deeply in the sufferings of Christ. He, too, felt that his Father had forsaken Him.

But for the rest of us who are a long way from that most intimate fellowship, there is another, much more common reason for darkness. We find it in the Psalms (107:10, 11 NEB): "Some sat in darkness, dark as death, prisoners bound fast in iron, because they had rebelled against God's commands, and flouted the purpose of the Most High."

Before we dignify our own experience of darkness by identifying it with the classic mystic experience, it might be well to see if we have not disobeyed the Lord in some way, or have been angry at Him because his purpose has been at odds with our cherished plans. Remember the saga of Israel's journey to the promised land—there were some difficulties along the way for which the Israelites railed against God. What they overlooked was the fact that his goal for them was a rich land where their every dream would come true.

Thank you, Lord, for your promise: "I am the light of the world. No follower of mine shall wander in the dark; he shall have the light of life" (Jn 8:12 NEB). □

# 5 Realities

"FAITH...MAKES US CERTAIN of realities we do not see" (Heb 11:1 NEB).

What realities can we be sure of? There is a popular notion about prayer which assumes that the thing asked for ought to be the object of faith—"Lord, give me this or that," wherefore "this" and "that" become the realities. No. The Bible states the absolutes that we can be certain of: the character of God, his love, his will that we be conformed to his Son's likeness, his sovereign control of all the universe. When faith latches on to those realities which we do not see with our eyes, it can never be confounded. If it makes the thing asked for its object, faith itself will dissolve if the Lord's answer is no, or not yet, or wait.

"In Thee, O Lord, do I put my trust. Let me never be put to confusion" (Ps 71:1 AV).  □

# 6 No Sand

AROUND THE TURN of the century an expression was used which today would be grit, guts, or gumption. A man was said to have "sand."

An unbeliever named Miller approached Mr. Frank Sandford with the scornful remark, "Jesus didn't have any sand."

"Didn't he? Well, He stretched out one hand and said to his captors, 'Put a spike in there for Miller!' Then he stretched out the other hand and said, 'Put another spike in there for Miller!' I don't know if you have enough sand to follow Him, but don't say He didn't have any sand."

Lord, give me sand enough to take up the cross daily and follow You. Help me to take lightly this world's judgments and to take seriously your call and your cross.  □

# 7 God's Messengers

HOW CAN *this* person who so annoys or offends me be God's messenger? Is God so unkind as to send *that* sort across my path? Insofar as his treatment of me requires more kindness than I can find in my own heart, demands love of a quality I do not possess, asks of me patience which only the Spirit of God can produce in me, he is God's messenger. God sends him in order that he may send me running to God for help.

The Psalms are full of cries to God about enemies—but it was the enemies that drove the psalmist (for example, in Psalm 64) to cry. If he had had no enemies, he would have had no need of a Protector. God will go to any lengths to bring us to Himself.

"Think of him who submitted to such opposition from sinners: that will help you not to lose heart and grow faint. . . . You have not yet resisted to the point of shedding your blood. . . . The Lord disciplines those whom he loves" (Heb 12:3, 4, 6 NEB).  □

# 8 Who Is in Charge?

THE PEOPLE OF ISRAEL complained loudly against Moses for having brought them out into a wilderness where there was nothing to their liking. "Better to have died in Egypt!" they said.

"It was the *Lord* who brought you out," Moses told them (Ex 16:6-8). "It is against the *Lord* that you bring your complaints, and not against us."

When we are angry or offended, let us be careful to note where our real complaint lies. This person who insults me at the office or on the bus, this husband who rides roughshod over my feelings, this insensitive individual who does not understand or appreciate me—is he not one whom God has put in my life for my good? Who, after all, is really in charge?

Let us beware of rebellion against the Lord. Circumstances are of his choosing, because He wants to bless us, to lead us (even through the wilderness) out of Egypt, that is, *out* of *ourselves*. Settle the complaint with God, and it will settle other things. Be offended with God, and you will be offended with everyone who crosses your path.  □

# 9 *Leave Him to Me*

WHEN THERE IS DEEP misunderstanding which has led to the erection of barriers between two who once were close, every day brings the *strengthening* of those barriers if they are not, by God's grace, breached. One prays and finds no way at all to break through. Love seems to "backfire" every time. Explanations become impossible. New accusations arise, it seems, from nowhere (though it is well to recall who is named the Accuser of the brethren). The situation becomes ever more complex and insoluble, and the mind goes round and round, seeking the place where things went wrong, brooding over the words which were like daggers, regretting the failures and mistakes, wondering (most painfully) how it *could* have been different. Much spiritual and emotional energy is drained in this way—but the Lord wants to teach us to commit, trust, and rest.

"Leave him to me this afternoon," is what his word is. "There is nothing else that I am asking of you *this* afternoon but that: leave him to Me. You cannot fathom all that is taking place. You don't need to. I am at work—in you, in him. Leave him to Me. Some day it will come clear—trust Me."

"Humble yourselves under God's mighty hand, and he will lift you up in due time. Cast all your cares on Him, for you [and the other] are his charge" (1 Pt 5:7).  □

# 10 My Own Canoe

"THE RULE OF THE UNIVERSE," wrote C. S. Lewis to his friend Arthur Greeves, is "that others can do for us what we cannot do for ourselves, and one can paddle every canoe *except* one's own" (*They Stand Together: The Letters of C. S. Lewis to Arthur Greeves*, p. 514).

This is grace—God graciously doing for us what we cannot do and so constructing human life that we are allowed to help—i.e., to give life to others. In our pride we try to save ourselves, but it is impossible. We can only lose by trying. It is when we stop straining to paddle our own canoe and let Another paddle it for us, or give ourselves to paddle someone else's ("bearing his burdens") that we fulfill the law of Christ. The wind carries the seed, the bee the pollen, the mother the child. So life is borne and born.  □

# 11 He Will If You Will

ALL THROUGH THE BIBLE we see the interworking of the will of God and the will of man. It was God, Creator and Sovereign, who conceived freedom for man—the glorious likeness to Himself in "the dignity of causality," to use Pascal's phrase. All things are so arranged in God's universe that He may work his will through man's exercising his gift of a free will. It *is* a gift, and one which, while it confers staggering power on us humans, also limits the Almighty. Here lies the tremendous mystery—that God should be all-powerful, yet refuse to coerce. He summons us to cooperation. We are honored in being given the opportunity to participate in his good deeds. Remember how He asked for help in performing his miracles: Fill the waterpots, stretch out your hand, distribute the loaves.

This little word of Paul's to the Corinthian Christians contains the whole kernel of that truth: "He will deliver us if you will cooperate by praying" (2 Cor 1:11).

Is there something you are hoping for today? Perhaps there is a condition *you* must fulfill before the Lord can grant it. *He* will if *you* will.  □

# 12  He Could Not Because They Would Not

THE OTHER SIDE of the coin of this amazing matter of cooperation with God is that there are things even God cannot do. He cannot because He has chosen to assign certain powers to his people. If they will not, his hands are tied.

"He did not many mighty works there because of their unbelief" (Mt 13:58 AV).

"How often would I have gathered you . . . but ye would not" (Mt 23:37 AV).

Some would argue that although it is proper to say that God will not and does not, it is not proper to say that He cannot. I would reply that given the terms of his relationship to us, the people He loved and called, He *cannot* force us, for He *cannot* deny Himself. To force us would be to deprive us of the freedom He granted when He made us, and thus to deny Himself.

Yet we pray, "Make me to do Thy will!" And so we should, for in that prayer we express our will to cooperate with Him.

"Our wills are ours to make them Thine." (Tennyson)  □

# 13 Who Am I?

THIS WAS MOSES' QUESTION when God said He would send him to Pharaoh to bring release for the enslaved Israelites. The early part of Moses' life shows him to be a champion—that is, a defender and protector (of the man being wronged, of the shepherd girls), but this was not the strength he was to depend on. The real question for Moses, as for us, is not "Who am I?" but, Who is it who summons us? It is the Lord, the I AM, the same yesterday, and today, and forever. He is *with* us. This is what matters. This is our reason for confidence.

Today we may find ourselves summoned to a task which we know is quite beyond us. "Me, Lord?" we quaver, "Who am I?" God answers, "I am with you."

The Lord of Hosts is with us
The God of Jacob is our refuge. (Ps 46:11 AV)  □

# 14 The Glory of God

WHEN GOD'S POWER is manifested in the world, in his creation, or in his people, God is glorified. When we pray that our lives may glorify Him, we are asking that the self may be put down, for it is not possible to show the power of God and at the same time to glorify what George MacDonald called "the bastard self." We must be prepared to *lose* ourselves, whatever that may entail, that God may be all in all. Losing an argument for his sake, losing something we held dear, losing "face," reputation, a position of power or superiority, losing a claim on someone or on his affection or respect—can these be a part of the answer to our prayer to glorify God in our lives? Assuredly they can, for assuredly the Son Himself laid aside all such assets when He came to do the will of the Father.

"I have glorified Thee on the earth".(Jn 17:4 AV), He said—and that *glory* was manifested through weakness, loss, and suffering. What a privileged position we are called to share.

Lord, lift up our eyes, away from ourselves and our small losses, up to that glory yet to be revealed. Teach us that it is only out of weakness that we are made strong, only as we suffer that we may reign, only as we lose that we may gain. ☐

# 15 A Bondslave of Christ

ABRAHAM WAS A VERY wealthy man who had many servants. He himself, knowing well what makes a good servant, was a faithful and obedient servant of God.

Nowadays most of us have never had servants and therefore have almost no notion of what it means to be one. It means first of all to have a master—that is, to belong to someone else. He can do what he wants with you; you are there to do for him. You are at his disposal. It is not for you to reason why he asks something of you; it is yours only to do it. So long as you are in his service, you are not your own (1 Cor 6:20).

Abraham was a man full of faith, obedient to his Lord, readily at his command.

Master, help me to live today according to your desires, and when I reach home may You be able to say, "Well done, good and faithful servant." ☐

# 16 *Watching Quietly, Praying Silently*

THE MAN WHOM ABRAHAM SENT to find a wife for his son Isaac had been long in Abraham's service. No doubt he had learned much of trust and obedience through watching his master walk with God. He set out on his mission, confident that God would help him. Beside the Well of Aram of Two Rivers he halted his camels and was praying silently when a beautiful young woman appeared with her water jar on her shoulder. She responded to his request as he had prayed she would, and he watched quietly to see whether the Lord had made his journey successful (Gn 24:21).

Very possibly we often miss what God wants to show us because we don't take time to pray silently and watch quietly. It was by doing those two things, along with the obvious practical things (let us not leave those undone) that the servant was able to say, "I have been guided by the Lord" (Gn 24:27 NEB). □

# 17 *Pedestals*

A STUDENT ASKED ME whether I thought it was a "problem" that we tend to place missionaries on pedestals. My answer was that indeed we do, but servants of the Lord *ought* to be models of the truth they proclaim. Paul was bold enough to say, "Be followers of me" (1 Cor 4:16).

At the same time let us always remember that the "excellency of the power" (2 Cor 4:7 AV) is never ours but God's. It is foolish to imagine that the missionary, or whoever the hero is, is sinless. God uses sinners—there is no one else to use.

Pedestals are for statues. Usually statues commemorate people who have done something admirable. Is the deed worth imitating? Does it draw me out of myself, set my sights higher? Let me remember the Source of all strength ("The Lord is the strength of my life," says Ps 27:1 AV) and, cheered by the image of a human being in whom that strength was shown, follow his example.  □

## 18 Invisible Blessings

BEING VERY MUCH of the earth—earthy—we always want tangible, visible things—proofs, demonstrations, something to latch onto. If we always had them, of course, faith would be "struck blind." When Jesus hung on a cross, the challenge was flung at Him: Come down! He stayed nailed, not so that spectators would be satisfied (that miracle, his coming down, would have been a great crowd-pleaser), but that the world might be *saved.*

Many of our prayers are directed toward the quick and easy solution. Long-suffering is sometimes the only means by which the greater glory of God will be served, and this is, for the moment, invisible. We must persist in faith. God *has* a splendid purpose. Believe in order to see it.

"Our troubles are slight and short-lived, and their outcome an eternal glory which outweighs them far. Meanwhile our eyes are fixed, not on the things that are seen, but on the things that are unseen" (2 Cor 4:17, 18 NEB).  □

## 19 Exchange

THIS MORNING I WAS THINKING of a friend who is gravely ill. She is greatly loved by many and has had a unique ministry because of her gifts of friendship and hospitality. *Must* she suffer?

The answer is yes. For the Lord who loves her suffered and wants her to fellowship with Himself. The joy of thus knowing Him comes not *in spite of* but *because* of suffering, just as resurrection comes out of death. I have a Savior because I am a sinner, and beauty is given the child of God in exchange for ashes.

We want to avoid suffering, death, sin, ashes. But we live in a world crushed and broken and torn, a world God Himself visited to redeem. We receive his poured-out life, and being allowed the high privilege of suffering with Him, may then pour ourselves out for others.

How can one's illness help another? By being offered to Him who can transform it into blessing.

"You have been granted the privilege not only of believing in Christ but also of suffering for Him" (Phil 1:29 NEB).  □

# 20 Wastelands

THERE ARE DRY, fruitless, lonely places in each of our lives, where we seem to travel alone, sometimes feeling as though we must surely have lost the way. What am *I* doing *here*? How did this happen? Lord, get me *out* of this!

He does not get us out. Not when we ask for it, at any rate, because it was He all along who brought us to this place. He has been here before—it is no wilderness to Him, and He walks with us. There are things to be seen and learned in these apparent wastelands which cannot be seen and learned in the "city"—in places of comfort, convenience, and company.

God does not intend to make it *no* wasteland. He intends rather to keep us—to hold us with his strength, to sustain us with his sure words—in a place where there is nothing else we can count on.

"God did not guide them by the road towards the Philistines, although that was the shortest. . . . God made them go round by way of the wilderness towards the Red Sea" (Ex 13:17, 18 NEB).

Imagine what Israel and all of us who worship Israel's God would have missed if they had gone by the short route—the thrilling story of the deliverance from Egypt's chariots when the sea was rolled back. Let's not ask for shortcuts. Let's keep alert for the wonders our Guide will show us in the wilderness. □

## 21  All Things Serve Thee

THE LORD'S DECREES (his promises, his plans, his every word) stand fast, no matter what news we receive. A child has run away. A mother has cancer. A business has failed. The events in our private lives and the great catastrophes in the world do not budge the solid ground on which the Christian takes his position. How can this be? Are there not conditions which harm and hinder and destroy? Not in the end. There is nothing, on earth or in hell or heaven, in time or in eternity, which can alter in any final sense what God has promised—because *all things* serve Him.

A word in the Book of the Revelation shows this truth most gloriously. Ten great kings will join their powers with an enormously powerful beast to wage war on the Lamb. God does not intervene to prevent that war.

"But the Lamb will defeat them, for He is Lord of Lords and King of Kings, and his victory will be shared by His followers, called and chosen and faithful" (Rv 17:14 NEB).

All things serve Him. That is, everything will at last be seen to be under his control, contributing to his eternal purposes— and (here is another marvel) the Lamb's victory will be *ours* as well.

Lord, who has called and chosen us—make us faithful. Enable us to keep our eyes on the final victory. □

## 22 A Mansion Prepared

JESUS TOLD HIS DISCIPLES of the place He was going to prepare for them. The collect for the fourth Sunday in Advent reminds us of the place we ought to prepare for Him: "Purify our conscience, Almighty God, by your daily visitation, that your Son Jesus Christ, at His coming, may find in us a mansion prepared for Himself."

A mansion in *me* for *Him*? What sort of mansion must it be? It must be swept clean of all evil, a task we cannot do by ourselves, but only by receiving daily the grace of God in ridding our conscience of guilt.

> Come—not to find, but make this troubled heart
> A dwelling worthy of Thee as Thou art.
> (Bishop Handley Moule)    □


## 23 A Chance to Die

TO BE TRANSFORMED into the image of Christ I must learn his character, love his obedience to the will of the Father, and begin, step by step, to walk the same pathway. For Christ the pathway of obedience began with emptying Himself. I must begin at the same place.

He "made Himself nothing." (Phil 2:7 NEB)

"You must arm yourselves with a temper of mind like His."
(1 Pt 4:1 NEB)

"If anyone wishes to be a follower of mine, he must leave self behind." (Mt 16:24 NEB)

What does this mean? Is it mere words? How can one leave self behind, make himself nothing? The answer will not come in a vacuum. If a man or woman honestly wishes to be a follower, the opportunity will present itself. Christ will say, "Here is your chance. Now, in this situation, you must make your choice. Will it be self? Or will you choose Me?"

An older missionary said something to Amy Carmichael when she was a young missionary that stayed with her for life. She had spoken of something which was not to her liking. His reply was, "See in it a chance to die."  □

## 24 The Right Clothes

ONLY CERTAIN COSTUMES suit Christians. To be otherwise dressed is inappropriate.

> "*Put on* the garments that suit God's chosen people, his own, his beloved: compassion, kindness, humility, gentleness, patience" (Col 3:12 NEB).

> "*Put on* the Lord Jesus Christ." (Rom 13:14 RSV)

> "You have all *put on* Christ as a garment." (Gal 3:27 NEB)

> "You must *put on* the new nature of God's creating."
> (Eph 4:24 NEB)

> "You have discarded the old nature with its deeds and have *put on* the new nature." (Col 3:10 NEB)

> "*Put on* love." (Col 3:14 RSV)

The clothes we wear are what people see. Only God can look on the heart. The outward signs are important. They reveal something of what is inside. If charity is there, it will become visible outwardly, but if you have no charitable feelings, you can still obey the command. Put it on as simply and consciously as you put on a coat. You choose it; you pick it up; you put it on. This is what you want to wear.

Do you want to dress like a Christian? Put on Christ. The act of honest obedience—the fruit of love for Christ—is your part. Making you Christlike through and through is his part. ☐

## 25 Outlandish Teachings

THERE IS NO END to the "new" methods offered for success, self-realization, fulfillment, understanding, and happiness. Seminars, conferences, and workshops abound. Go to so-and-so, get counseling, a new exercise program, a new diet, another degree, job, husband, house, color scheme. If it's new, it's good.

Jesus Christ is the same, yesterday, today, and forever. "Do not be swept off your course by all sorts of outlandish teachings; it is good that our souls should gain their strength from the grace of God" (Heb 13:8, 9 NEB).

Fixity of heart is a rare thing and probably always has been. It is easier to follow after the world in its futile pursuit of happiness, simply because we are like sheep and we go astray. To stay quietly by the Shepherd seems harder, but in the end we find there (and nowhere else) our soul's real strength.

Pascal wrote, "I have discovered that all the unhappiness of man arises from one single fact, that they cannot stay quietly in their own chamber." Try spending a half hour in a room alone, without music, without television, without even reading. Can you find any peace or happiness there? If not, perhaps you have not begun to learn what is truly important. ☐

## 26 What Makes God's Work Shine

BROTHER MASSEO ASKED St. Francis of Assisi why all the world should go running after him who was neither handsome nor learned nor even of noble birth. At this, Francis was overjoyed, and after kneeling to thank God, said, "Why me? Why me? The all-seeing God, looking down and finding nothing viler on earth, quite naturally fixed His gaze on me. For to make His work shine forth in men's eyes, the Lord takes what is learned, strong, and noble, so that the glory may go to the sole Author of all good."

We are only pots—common ones of clay, so that the splendid power may belong to God and not to us (2 Cor 4:7 NEB).  □


## 27 Nothing Is Lost

PAUL WAS A MAN who suffered the loss of everything, according to his own claim. Yet any loss he counted pure gain. The key to this transforming of earthly losses into heavenly gains is love. What do we love? If our hearts are set on people and possessions and position, the loss of those will indeed be irreparable. To the man or woman whose heart is set on Christ no loss on earth can be irreparable. It may shock us for the moment. We may feel hurt, outraged, desolate, helpless. That is our humanity. But the Lord can show us the "long view," the incalculable gain in spiritual and eternal terms, if we love Him above all. Everything that belongs to us belongs also to Him. Everything that belongs to Him belongs also to us. What, then, can we *finally* lose? If we lose not Christ Himself, we have finally lost nothing, for He is our treasure and He has our hearts.  □

# 28 The Token of Integrity

"WITH A SERVANT, a warrior, a child, a subject," writes Andrew Murray in *The New Life*, "obedience is indispensable, the first token of integrity."

God is my Master, my Captain, my Father, my King. I am servant, warrior, child, subject. What have I to do in any of these cases but obey?

Integrity means wholeness, unbroken condition, the quality of being unimpaired and sound. An integer is something which is complete in itself, an entity. No one can serve two masters. Divided loyalty will mean impaired obedience. "A soldier on active service will not let himself be involved in civilian affairs; he must be wholly at his commanding officer's disposal" (2 Tm 2:4 NEB).

O Christ, be Master and Captain of my life. Give me a whole heart united to do your bidding and to do nothing else. Let me hear your voice and no other. Make my life an integer for your glory. Amen. ☐

# 29 The Work of the Accuser

ONE OF THE NAMES of the enemy is the Accuser. It is his doing, when we have sought God's guidance and been as obedient as we knew how, and then remain in an agony of doubt as to whether God *did* guide, whether we really *did* obey. There is no end to the "proofs" the Accuser can present to sow doubt in our minds. "Hath God said?" (Gn 3:1 AV) was the first seed he sowed in the mind of Eve, and he has had a great deal of practice at that kind of planting ever since.

It is to be expected that every decision made with the desire to be obedient to God will be attacked. Spread your doubts before the Lord. Pray for correction of any wrong in thinking or doing and for his word of assurance as to the action you must take. If there is nothing else required of you *at this moment,* leave it at that. Trust God. Put the whole weight of your doubts and cares on Him—that will foil the Accuser.

"It is God who pronounces our acquittal. . . . It is Christ who pleads . . . our cause" (Rom 8:33, 34 NEB).  □

# 30 *Man of Dust*

"AS WE HAVE WORN the likeness of the man made of dust, so we shall wear the likeness of the heavenly man" (1 Cor 15:49 NEB).

What a word of hope for us when we are discouraged with our own sinfulness! The old Adam is always there, rising in rebellion against the new life which Christ has given us. There is constant struggle, daily reminders that we are yet very unholy, very un-Christlike, very dusty. But a day will come when even I, with all my glaring faults, will *wear the likeness* of the heavenly Man. This gives me ammunition to fire at the Accuser. I *shall* be like Christ—just wait! You'll see!  □

# 31 *Out of All Proportion*

WHEN MY HUSBAND was near death from cancer, depression often seemed to overwhelm him like great black waves, and he was at times convinced (we know the source of this conviction) that his sins were unforgivable.

"Do you really think God can forgive *my* sins?" he would ask, for he felt that his sins were out of all proportion to the light that had been given him as a Christian (a Christian home, a Christian education, a wide sphere of Christian service).

The popular notion of somehow "balancing" our good deeds against our sins will not hold much reassurance for any of us when we face the final truth. Then we need grace, infinite grace, and plenty of it.

It is there for us—mighty waves, deeper and stronger than our blackest despair.

I had to remind my husband of what he knew very well intellectually: that his particular sins could not possibly exhaust the grace of God.

"God's act of grace is *out of all* proportion" to our wrongdoing (Rom 5:15 NEB). □

## MONTH TWO

# 1 Volunteer Slaves

"SLAVE" IS NOT A WORD most of us nowadays "feel comfortable" with. It is significant that most modern Bible translations use "servant" instead. For a slave is not his own, has no rights whatsoever, is not in charge of what happens to him, makes no choices about what he will do or how he is to serve, is not recognized, appreciated, thanked or even (except by his absence) noticed at all.

Once we give up our slavery to the world, which is a cruel master indeed, to become Christ's bondslave, we live out our servitude to Him by glad service to others. This volunteer slavery cannot be taken advantage of—we have chosen to surrender everything for love. It is a wholly different thing from forced labor. It is in fact the purest joy when it is most unobserved, most unself-conscious, most simple, most freely offered.

Lord, break the chains that hold me to myself; free me to be your happy slave—that is, to be the happy foot-washer of anyone today who needs his feet washed, his supper cooked, his faults overlooked, his work commended, his failure forgiven, his griefs consoled, or his button sewed on. Let me not imagine that my love for You is very great if I am unwilling to do for a human being something very small. ◻

## 2 Pray Hard, Work Tirelessly

SOMETIMES WE THINK of these two things as in opposition. The Bible never places them so, but shows how perfectly they harmonize. Prayer is one kind of work, necessary to the proper doing of all other kinds. When we pray, we are in touch with God, expectant, trusting: *He* is at work. *He* does what we *cannot* do. *We* are to be at work also, doing what we can do.

In Paul's closing remarks to the Christians in Colossae he includes greetings from Epaphras.

He prays hard for you all the time....
He works tirelessly for you. (Col 4:12 NEB)

As we pray, the Lord frequently shows us what we ourselves can do to cooperate with Him in bringing about the answer. Let us *listen* as we pray. Then let us go out and work tirelessly. ◻

## 3 From Start to Finish

THE GREAT WITNESSES to faith in the eleventh chapter of Hebrews, beginning with Abel, who offered a sacrifice by faith, down to those nameless others whose stories are not success stories by any stretch of the imagination, did not know Jesus, God's full revelation of Himself. Yet they believed. Yet they were strong in faith. It was, although they were ignorant of it, Christ on whom their faith rested. Faith depends on Him "from start to finish" (Heb 12:2 NEB). The whole saga of human faith from Abel to us in the twentieth century depends on Him who endured a cross. The whole story of any one individual's faith also depends on Him from start to finish. There is no other ground anywhere. He is the Rock.

I don't know why I keep forgetting this and assuming that somewhere along the line (or the racetrack) I am supposed to manage it by myself. It is Jesus at the start, Jesus every foot of the track, Jesus at the finish. Trust *Him*. Trust *Him*. Trust *Him*.

So, through life, death, through sorrow and through sinning
Christ shall suffice me, for He hath sufficed.
Christ is the End, for Christ was the Beginning—
Christ the Beginning, for the End is Christ.
(F.W.H. Meyer, St. Paul)  □

# 4 His Blood and My Conscience

IN THE CONSCIENCE of all of us sinners there is *deadness* from our former ways. This has its effect on our present behavior, in ways we little realize, and hinders our fitness for service to God. But there is a remedy: the power of the blood of Christ.

"His blood will cleanse our conscience from the deadness of our former ways and fit us for the service of the living God" (Heb 9:14 NEB).

This morning I was troubled about what seemed to be a blockage deep down where I could not get at it. I was glad it was not too deep or too strong for the power of the blood to reach and cleanse. Satan would try to convince me daily that I am full of "hang-ups" which unfit me for God's service. The blood of Christ is my answer to his challenge. It will never lose its power.  □

## 5 What Fits Us for Service

IS THERE ANY CHRISTIAN who does not long for some special experience, vision, or feeling of the presence of God? This morning it seemed to me that unless I could claim such I was merely going through motions of prayer, meditation, reading; that the book I am writing on discipline will prove to be nothing but vanity and a striving after wind. The Lord brought yesterday's word to mind again with this emphasis: it is not any *experience*, no matter how exciting, not any vision, however vivid and dazzling, not any feeling, be it ever so deep that fits me for service. It is the power of the blood of Christ. I am "made holy by the single unique offering of the body of Jesus Christ" (Heb 10:10), and by his blood "fit for the service of the living God." My spiritual numbness cannot cancel that—the blood will *never lose its power.* ☐

## 6 Saving Ourselves

TODAY I WAS TEMPTED in a new way (the Tempter has a bag of many tricks) to "save" myself. This time it involved a matter of "face." The Lord reminded me that I should let it go.

We are always trying to save ourselves in one way or another. It is impossible, except on the terms Jesus gave the disciples: let yourself be lost (Mt 16:25 NEB). It was the only way Jesus could save the world, though the people challenged Him to save Himself. "Himself He cannot save" (Mk 15:31 AV) was what they said, uttering an eternal principle far deeper than they had any idea of. It is true for us as well. If we are going to obey the will of the Father, we cannot save ourselves. We must give ourselves up, be lost—*then*, and only then, will we "find" ourselves.

Lord, deliver me from the faithless desire for self-preservation when obedience to You requires self-abandonment. □

## 7 Death Is a Gateway to the Palace

TO BE A CHRISTIAN is to be a subject—subject to a king—that is, to welcome the rule of God in one's life. Jesus Himself became subject to the Father—"Lo, I come to do Thy will, O God" (Heb 10:7 AV). This meant that He had come to this world, not to gain, but to lose; not to get, but to give; not to be served, but to serve; not to obtain bread but to *be* bread, the Bread of heaven, broken for the life of the world.

"Let this mind be in you which was also in Christ Jesus.... He humbled Himself" (Phil 2:5-8 AV).

That puts it in very simple terms. If you want to be a Christian, see that your mind is made up as his was: be humble, be subject, be obedient—even to *death*. It will mean death. Be sure of that. Death to some of your desires and plans at least. Death to *yourself*. But never forget—Jesus' death was what opened the way for his own exaltation and our everlasting *Life*. Our death to selfishness is the shining gateway into the glories of the palace of the King. Is it so hard to be his subject? Is the price too high? □

## 8 Immunity—No. Grace—Yes

SOMEONE ASKED LAST WEEK, "When Jim died was your walk with the Lord close enough that his love and comfort and presence were sufficient at all times—or did grief and sorrow at times overtake and overwhelm you?"

My answer is yes to both questions. It is not an either-or

matter. The psalmist, overwhelmed, prayed, "Lead me to the Rock that is higher than I" (Ps 61:2 AV).

Paul, plagued by a thorn, besought the Lord three times to remove it.

Jesus, "horror-stricken and desperately depressed," prayed "O My Father—if it be possible . . ." (Mk 14:34, 36).

Of none of these—the psalmist, the apostle, the Lord—could it be said that his walk with God was not close enough. There was human suffering and divine sufficiency. This is the story of our life. The promise is "My grace is *sufficient*" (2 Cor 12:9 AV), not "My grace will abolish your thorns."  □

# 9 *How to Know God*

THE ORDER OF THE Christian's assignment is: hear, do, know. If we hear the commandments and obey them, the Father will make Himself known to us. It is no use trying to know Him without doing what He says. To listen to one word and go out and obey it is better than having the most exalted "religious experience," for it puts us in touch with God Himself—it is a willed response.

"If you really love me you will keep the commandments I have given you." It is perilously easy to imagine that we love God because we like the idea of God, or because we feel drawn to Him. The only valid test of love is obedience. Take one thing commanded and start doing it. Take one thing forbidden and stop doing it. Then we are on the sure road to knowing God. There is no other.

"You are my friends, if you do what I command you" (Jn 15:14 NEB).

"The man who has received my commands and obeys them—he it is who loves me: and he who loves me will be loved by my Father; and I will love him and disclose myself to him" (Jn 14:21). There is the order: hear, do, know.  □

# 10 Let Thy Words Be Few

A CHRISTIAN BUSINESSMAN who served on the board of a college with my father told me what sort of board member my father was. He would wait until others had had their say and would then rise. He felt it was important to stand, though others did not usually do so, in order to be heard clearly. With a few well-chosen words he would then state his own position. He could be counted on to say more in these few words, and to say it more clearly and simply, than any of the others. My friend said he found himself waiting for what my father would say.

I knew from our home training how valuable time was to him. He was deeply conscientious not to waste it, whether it was his own or (especially) others'.

He did not like to waste words. They were tools to be used skillfully and carefully.

"God is in heaven and thou upon earth, therefore let thy words be few" (Eccl 5:2 AV).  □

# 11 The Necessity to Cover

THERE ARE THINGS which it is our duty to cover in silence. We are told nowadays that everything ought to be expressed if we are truly "honest" and "open."

Proverbs 11:13 says, "He who goes abroad as a talebearer reveals secrets, but he who is trustworthy in spirit keeps a thing hidden."

Jesus sometimes refused to reveal the truth about Himself, even when it would have seemed to us "an opportunity to witness." He did not always answer questions. He did not always say who He was. He told some of those He healed to tell no one about it.

"For every activity under heaven its time . . . a time for silence and a time for speech" (Eccl 3:1, 7 NEB). "A man of understanding remains silent" (Prv 11:12 RSV).

Lord, deliver me from the urge to open my mouth when I should shut it. Give me the wisdom to keep silence where silence is wise. Remind me that not everything needs to be said, and that there are very few things that need to be said *by me*. ☐

## 12 *The Hope of Holiness*

THE "OPENNESS" that is often praised among Christians as a sign of true humility may sometimes be an oblique effort to prove that there is no such thing as a saint after all, and that those who believe that it is possible in the twentieth century to live a holy life are only deceiving themselves. When we enjoy listening to some Christian confess his weaknesses and failures, we may be eager only to convince ourselves that we are not so bad after all. We sit on the edge of our chairs waiting to grasp at an excuse for continuing to do what we have made up our minds long ago to do anyway. The Lord is ready to forgive sin at any moment and to make strong servants out of the worst of us. But we must believe it; we must come to Him in faith for forgiveness and deliverance and then go out to do the work He has given us to do.

"Charity rejoiceth not in iniquity" (1 Cor 13:6 AV). Let us be willing to call *iniquity* what is really iniquity, rather than to call it weakness, temperament, failure, hangups, or to fall back on the tired excuse, "It's just the way I am."

Create in me a clean heart, O God,
And renew a right spirit within me. (Ps 51:10 AV) ☐

# 13 All Things Serve Thee

DURING MY HUSBAND ADDISON'S terminal illness, everything in our lives was changing. The cancer had spread with a speed which startled the doctors. I found during those hard days and nights strength in the ringing words of the liturgy, proclaimed aloud as the congregation knelt: "Christ has died. Christ has risen. Christ will come again." I could hold onto those immutable facts.

The psalmist found the same strength in the Lord's infrangible decrees: "This day, as ever, Thy decrees stand fast: for all things serve Thee" (Ps 119:91 NEB). The Lord is not subject to vicissitudes, exigencies, and contingencies. "Accidents" are, in fact, subject to the Lord of the universe, the blessed Controller of all things.

"Thy promise endures for all time, stable as the earth which Thou hast fixed" (Ps 119:90 NEB).

He "fixes," that is, He sets in place, the whole earth. Surely He can fix and establish my heart. Every "happening" *serves* Him. □

# 14 Hidden Work

FEW OF US ACCOMPLISH without delay or interruption what we set out to accomplish. Plans are made, and they fail. We dream dreams, and they are not fulfilled. Even what seem to be soberly realistic schedules are interrupted by unforeseen demands. Often we are tempted to quit our efforts altogether, to take a careless attitude, or to give in to helplessness, despair, and frustration.

When the apostle Paul's itinerant ministry was brought to a standstill by his imprisonment in Rome, he had plenty of human reasons for giving up. He wrote to the Christians at Philippi, who themselves were suffering persecution, reminding them of the humble obedience of Christ. "You too, my friends, must be obedient, as always.... You must work out your own salvation in fear and trembling; for it is God who works in you, inspiring both the will and the deed, for his own chosen purpose. Do all you have to do without complaint or wrangling" (Phil 2:12-14 NEB).

Imprisonments, persecutions, late planes, an attack of the flu, an uninvited guest, or an unpleasant confrontation—never mind. Be obedient as always! Such a simple directive. So hard to carry out—*unless* we also remember that we are not by any means alone in our effort. God also is at work in us, always accomplishing what we could not accomplish if left to ourselves: his own chosen purpose. □

## 15 Tit for Tat

HE THAT WOULD HAVE FRIENDS must show himself friendly.

If you sow sparingly, you will get a scant harvest.

This is the way things generally work. There is another verse which falls into the same category but which, being sometimes interpreted as a command instead of a description, has led to confusion. "Pass no judgment and you will not be judged" (Mt 7:2 NEB). Jesus was not promising an escape from divine judgment for those who refrain from making judgments on others, nor was he asking us to suspend our critical faculties. He was simply pointing out the responsibility we assume when we judge. To say, for example, "Don't lie," or "Lying is a sin," is to lay oneself open to scrutiny in this matter. Do *I* lie? Is it sin for *me*? Be careful. Jesus said, "As you judge others, so you will yourselves be judged, and whatever measure you deal out to others will be dealt back to you" (Mt 7:1, 2 NEB). A willingness to submit to the same moral law by which we judge is the prerequisite for judgment.

In a time when every man does that which is right in his own eyes (or at least "feels good") it is no wonder we prefer to interpret Jesus' words as a command: "Judge not." We thus absolve ourselves of responsibility for making any moral distinctions in the behavior of others or of ourselves. "If I don't call what they do 'sin,' they can't call what I do 'sin.'"

This is comfortable for both of us. If I let him keep his "speck," he'll let me keep my "plank."

Jesus commanded us to remove both—the plank first, then the brother's speck. Submit, in other words, to treatment. Accept the consequences. To be judged is the consequence of judging, and to recognize one's own need is prerequisite. □

## 16 Obedience Is Not Contingent

THE MAKING OF COMPARISONS is a dangerous business for a Christian. Each of us must give account, not of his neighbor, but of himself to God. To the workers who, under the guise of a concern for fairness, objected to an equal wage being paid to those who began the job at different hours of the day, the owner said, "Why be jealous because I am kind?" (Mt 20:15 NEB).

To the brother of the prodigal son, put out because this wastrel was being wined and dined, the father said, "My boy, you are always with me, and everything I have is yours. How could we help celebrating this happy day?" (Lk 15:31, 32 NEB).

To Peter, hesitant to follow the Lord until he found out what was going to be required of the other disciple, Jesus said, "If it should be my will that he wait until I come, what is it to you? Follow me" (Jn 21:22 NEB).

The spirit of godly obedience is not in us; our wills have not been unconditionally turned over to the Master, as long as we determine our own action by what others do. To husbands God says (unconditionally), "Love your wives." To wives He says (unconditionally), "Submit to your husbands."* If each lets his obedience be contingent upon the other's, there is a standoff. The command to husbands is the business of husbands. The command to wives is the business of wives. Let each "mind his own"—direct his attention to the thing required of him—and harmony will be the result.

"There must be *no limit* to your goodness, as your heavenly Father's goodness knows no bounds" (Mt 5:48 NEB).  □

---

*Many wives consider their own cases exceptional. Since no exceptions are mentioned in this passage, I conclude that a wife must be very sure she has a scriptural warrant before disobeying, e.g., if her husband desires her to act in a way clearly forbidden by scripture.

## 17 Take Strength

THESE STRONG, SIMPLE WORDS can be spiritual adrenaline for us when we need them. They were written by a man who knew what he was talking about, as he himself was in prison. He was writing to a young minister who was also suffering and evidently tempted by doubt, fear, even uncertainty of his call. The older man admonishes him very lovingly to take his share of suffering, take his share of hardship like a good soldier, and to *take strength* from the grace of God (2 Tm 2:1 NEB).

Where shall I ever find the strength I need to get through this experience, this ordeal, this day, this week? The answer is Take it! Take it from the grace which *is ours* already, in Christ Jesus.

"Here it is," He is saying, "Will you have some?"

"Yes, thank You, Lord. I'll take it."  □

# 18 Give Way to Truth

THROUGH A DISAGREEMENT with my husband Lars yesterday I suddenly recognized an instrument used powerfully by the enemy to drive a wedge between two people who love each other (and there is nothing which fills the enemy with such glee as destroying unity). It is reason. I had good reasons for my argument and so did he. Reason comes very close to being an idol to me at times, and I am tempted to make sacrifices on its altar.

"Be faithful to Reason!" whispers the Destroyer. "Do not let go!"

"Be faithful to Me," Christ says, "give up your reasons, give way to Truth."

Reason is one of God's great gifts. We have intelligence and the faculty of reason, to be employed in the service of God and other people. Faithfulness to Christ (who *is* Truth) does not negate reason, but purifies it, raises it to a higher level.

"Pure" reason, logical argument, stood between my husband and me, as it stood between Job and his friends, and Jesus and the Pharisees.

"Knowledge gives self-importance—it is love that makes the building grow. A man may imagine that he understands something, but still not understand anything in the way he ought to!" (1 Cor 8:1, 2 JB).  □

# 19 We Do Not Belong to Darkness

THERE ARE TIMES when we cannot see our way, and it seems that darkness is about to overcome and hold us. It must have seemed so to the Christians in Thessalonica. Paul spoke of their grave suffering because of having welcomed his message. Must the coming of the light of God's truth bring suffering? Yes, often it does, and the one who has received it with joy is plunged into darkness. But darkness is *not* his master! He does not "belong" to it (1 Thes 5:6 NEB) but is in fact a "child of light," having been given word of things to come—resurrection, the sound of an archangel's voice, God's trumpet-call, the descent of the Lord Himself. "God has not destined us to the terrors of judgment.... He died for us so that we, awake or asleep, might live in company with Him" (5:9, 10). A small child is at peace even in the dark if his father or mother is with him. He has company. How different the darkness feels then.

Take the word of the Lord in your darkness. If He died to let us live in his company, is He likely to abandon us just because things look dark? ☐

## 20 *Hoping under the Lord Jesus*

WHEN PAUL WAS IN PRISON, he wrote a very beautiful letter to the Christians in Philippi, a letter full of joy, love, and tenderness. It contains many little human touches which give us glimpses of a Paul who is quite different from the popular image. Here we see not a stern and redoubtable theologian-authority figure, but a kind man with a simple and thoroughly childlike trust. His heart is warm and open to these dear friends who are so important to him as he lies in chains in his cell, his every human feeling utterly submitted to the Lord for whom he is glad to suffer. *Naturally* he hungers for news of them and hopes Timothy will be able to bring it. Even such a common human desire is placed matter-of-factly under the authority of his Master.

"I hope (under the Lord Jesus) to send Timothy."

If it is possible, if it works out, if it is God's will—even this small detail he offered to the Lord Jesus for his permission, like the psalmist who prayed, "Lord, all my desire is before Thee" (Ps 38:9 AV).

Let our hopes for today be *under the Lord Jesus*—screened by Him who loves us and can work them all out if they are good for us and for all concerned.  □

## 21 *What Was the Question?*

"CHRIST IS THE ANSWER" has been a wall motto, and, more recently, a bumper sticker. Somebody added, in small print, "What was the question?"

In the final analysis, it does not matter what question we are asking. All questions come under one of three headings:

1. Way—we need guidance
2. Truth—we need a norm
3. Life—we need sustenance.

Jesus said, "I am" all of these things. Let us bring everything that baffles us into his presence, holding it up before Him by faith. In that Light, the look of things will slowly begin to change, and as we humble ourselves to receive the true answer, our eyes will be opened. We learn to know Christ, then, as we walk in his way, obey his truth, and live his life. He Himself, a living, loving Person, *is* our answer.  □

## 22 *God's Secret Purpose*

WHATEVER THE ENEMY of our souls can do to instill doubt about the real purpose of the Father of our souls, he will certainly try to do. "Hath God said?" was his question to Eve, and she trusted him, the enemy, and doubted God. Each time the suspicion arises that God is really "out to get us," that He is bent on making us miserable or thwarting any good we might seek, we are calling Him a liar. His secret purpose has been revealed to us, and it is to bring us finally, not to *ruin*, but to *glory*. That is precisely what the Bible tells us: "His secret purpose framed from the very beginning [is] to bring us to our full glory" (1 Cor 2:7 NEB).

I know of no more steadying hope on which to focus my mind when circumstances tempt me to wonder why God doesn't "*do* something." He is always doing something—the very best thing, the thing we ourselves would certainly choose if we knew the end from the beginning. He is at work to bring us to our full glory.  □

## 23 *Discerning the Will of God*

THE PRIMARY CONDITION for learning what God wants of us is putting ourselves wholly at his disposal. It is just here that we are often blocked. We hold certain reservations about how far we are willing to go, what we will or will not do, how much God can have of us or of what we treasure. Then we pray for guidance. It will not work. We must begin by laying it all down—ourselves, our treasures, our destiny. Then we are in a position to think with renewed minds and act with a transformed nature. The withholding of any part of ourselves is the same as saying, "Thy will be done up to a point, mine from there on."

Paul gives four important steps to discerning the will of God:

1. "Offer your very selves to Him,"
2. "Adapt yourselves no longer to the pattern of this present world."
3. "Let your minds be remade."
4. "Your whole nature transformed."

"*Then* you will be able to discern the will of God" (Rom 12:1, 2 NEB).  □

## 24  No Love without Grief

*Tell us, fool, who knows more of love—the one who has joys from it or the one who has trials and griefs? He answered: There cannot be any knowledge of love without both of them.*

(Ramon Lull, *The Book of the Lover and the Beloved*)

WHEN I IMAGINE that I want to learn to love God—and to love my husband and others whom God has given me to love—let me test the desire of my willingness to accept trial and grief. If I can welcome them—*Yes, Lord!*—and believe God's purpose in them, I am learning the lesson of love. If I cannot, it's a fair indication that my desire to love is a delusion.  □


## 25  Rich Enough

THIS MORNING I WAS PRAYING about three very complicated matters for which I have a share of responsibility. I could not see my way through them and realized, as I prayed, that because I could not *see* a way, I was doubtful that there *was* a way. My limitations became, in my mind, God's limitations. Then my reading fell on Romans 10, where Paul speaks of the same sort of error (though much more far-reaching than mine)—that of the Jews having supposed that they must find the way of righteousness by themselves, and that Gentiles could not possibly find it. The way is and always has been God's and only God's, open to those who trust Him. For "the same Lord is Lord of all, and is rich enough for the need of all who invoke Him" (Rom 10:12 NEB).

"*Rich enough!*" I had been praying as though my own needs might exhaust God's resources.

Thou art coming to a King,
Large petitions with thee bring,
For His grace and power are such
None can ever ask too much.
            (John Newton)   □


## 26  Faith Is Holding Out Your Hand

SOMETIMES WHEN I WAS A CHILD my mother or father would say, "Shut your eyes and hold out your hand." That was the promise of some lovely surprise. I trusted them, so I shut my eyes instantly and held out my hand. Whatever they were going to give me I was ready to take. So it should be in our trust of our heavenly Father. Faith is the willingness to receive whatever He wants to give, or the willingness not to have what He does not want to give.

I am content to be and have what in Thy heart
I am meant to be and have.
    (George MacDonald, *Diary of an Old Soul*)

From the greatest of all gifts, salvation in Christ, to the material blessings of any ordinary day (hot water, a pair of legs that work, a cup of coffee, a job to do and strength to do it), every good gift comes down from the Father of Lights. Every one of them is to be received glady and, like gifts people give us, with thanks.

Sometimes we want things we were not meant to have. Because He loves us, the Father says no. Faith trusts that no. Faith is willing not to have what God is not willing to give. Furthermore, faith does not insist upon an explanation. It is enough to know his promise to give what is *good*—He knows so much more about that than we do.   □

# 27 What's My Score?

I WAS TEMPTED THIS MORNING—no, not merely tempted, I actually did it—to pray, "Lord, I've been disobedient in many things, but I've been obedient in the 'big' things, haven't I, Lord?"

"What would you call loving Me with all your heart, soul, mind, and strength? Is it a little thing?"

"Oh Lord, no."

"And is it a little thing to love your neighbor as yourself?"

"It is a very big thing, Lord—especially when I try to include you-know-who."

"These two things are all I require. Do them and you will have fulfilled all the law."

Silence. So much for my self-righteousness.

"Lord, have mercy on me, a sinner." □

# 28 The Desires of My Heart

I HAD BEEN PRAYING for something I wanted very badly. It seemed a good thing to have, a thing that would make life even more pleasant than it is, and would not in any way hinder my work. God did not give it to me. Why? I do not know all of his reasons, of course. The God who orchestrates the universe has a good many things to consider that have not occurred to me, and it is well that I leave them to Him. But one thing I do understand: He offers me holiness at the price of relinquishing my own will.

"Do you honestly want to know Me?" He asks. I answer yes. "Then do what I say," He replies. "Do it when you understand it; do it when you don't understand it. Take what I give you; be willing not to have what I do not give you. The very relinquishment of this thing that you so urgently desire is a true demonstration of the sincerity of your lifelong prayer: *Thy will be done.*

So instead of hammering on heaven's door for something which it is now quite clear God does not want me to have, I make my desire an offering. The longed-for thing is material for sacrifice. Here, Lord, it's yours.

He will, I believe, accept the offering. He will transform it into something redemptive. He may perhaps give it back as He did Isaac to Abraham, but He will know that I fully intend to obey Him.  □

## 29  I Will Not Be Afraid

NEWS REPORTS COME EVERY DAY concerning economic and political calamities about to befall us all, not to mention famines, tornadoes, earthquakes, and volcanoes, things which may at any moment strike us or people we love. There are always plenty of good reasons to be afraid—unless you know that things are under control. A Christian has this "inside information." Things are, in fact, under control. God is our Refuge, our Strength, our Mighty Fortress. Nothing will get by the moat of his protection without his permission. To be afraid of what happens today or what may happen tomorrow is not only an awful waste of energy, it is not only useless, it is disobedient. We are forbidden to fear anything but the Lord Himself.

When Christians in China were being hounded to death in the 1930s, one of them (I am told) wrote this simple song, which has helped me in countless times of fear ever since I learned it as a high school girl:

I will not be afraid.
I will not be afraid.
I will look upward, and travel onward,
And not be afraid.

Will power, of course, will not always overcome human emotions. But willed obedience to the One who is in charge, coupled with prayer for his help in vanquishing our natural fears, is something else.  □

## 30  *Leave the Results with God*

SCRIPTURE DOES NOT PROMISE that obedience to God will always be attended by earthly success and never by difficulties. Someone asked me again last week if I am not bothered by the negative results attending our opening up the Auca tribe to the gospel. "Of course I am bothered," I said. We messengers of the gospel are sinners like the Aucas—God has chosen to work through sinful human beings—and while we offer to them Bread and the Water of Life, which are priceless, we also introduce to them new varieties of sin and disease. We pray for protection from such things—for ourselves and for them. We must do the thing commanded—preach the gospel—and we must trust God for the results. If we wait until we are sure we shall do a thing purely and perfectly, we shall never accomplish the will of God on earth.

Negative results are not by any means always the fault of God's messengers. Recall the warnings Jesus gave his disciples when He sent them out to preach the kingdom—they could expect to be rejected, arrested, and flogged. Families would turn against each other. "I have not come to bring peace, but a sword," he said (Mt 10:34 NEB). Recall, too, the death of innocent infant boys as a result of the birth of One who the king feared might supplant him. God is engineering a master plan for good. Only He sees the end from the beginning.  □

# 31 The Danger of Not Knowing God

WE ARE MEANT TO BE WITNESSES for God—people who have seen and known Him and are willing to speak of what they see and know. Sometimes there is danger for such people—as in Russia, where it can mean forced labor, banishment, death. In China in the early 1930s a missionary couple, John and Betty Stam, were captured by Chinese Communists and marched through the streets of the village to a chopping block where each was beheaded. If they had been willing to recant their Christian faith, their lives would have been spared. Given their commitment to Christ, such a choice was unthinkable. They placed not only their lives but the life of their baby, Helen Priscilla, in the hands of God, confident that God could protect them if He chose, and, if He chose not to, it was safer to be in those hands than anywhere else in the universe. Like thousands of Christians before them, they preferred the sword to disobedience, believing that the danger of not knowing God is infinitely greater than any other danger.

Lord, be our Sun and Shield. Shine on us, protect us as we seek to live and witness to your truth. Forgive us (especially those of us who have never faced lions, fire, or sword because of our faith) for our fears of petty loss. Remind us that it is in losing ourselves that we find You. □

## MONTH THREE

# 1 Dispensers of Grace

EACH CHRISTIAN IS A DISPENSER. God has supplied each one with gifts He has selected (He does not offer an array of options), with the good of all in mind. When we imagine that these gifts are for our own mere satisfaction, we are forgetting they are intended for service. All that I have is meant to contribute to the needs of others, and what I need will be supplied through God's dispensers. Thus He unifies and harmonizes the whole church, which is his body, making each dispenser *indispensable*, for each dispenses a grace which is peculiarly his.

"Serve one another with the particular gifts God has given each of you, as faithful dispensers of the magnificently varied grace of God" (1 Pt 4:10 NEB). ☐


# 2 *Wait Quietly*

FEW OF US ENJOY HAVING to wait for something we want. It is human nature to desire instant gratification, and it is divine nature to do many things very, very slowly. Growth is always imperceptible. But the farmer exercises long patience in waiting for his crop. He has done his work and is assured of the result, hence he waits *quietly*. He is at rest because the outcome (barring disastrous "acts of God") is certain. If we could simply remember that this is true of everything—that God's purposes are slowly being worked out for his glory and our good—we would, like the farmer, keep faith and wait quietly.

Lord, take from us all fretting and hurrying and teach us to rest our hearts in the "ultimate certainty" (Jas 5:7 JBP). ☐


# 3 *Interrupted Plans*

WE LIKE THINGS TO GO SMOOTHLY and as planned. Very often unexpected things intervene, and our plans go awry. We think we've got "problems." There is another level at which everything that happens is being engineered. "God has no problems," Corrie ten Boom said, "only plans." When ours are interrupted, his are not. His plans are proceeding exactly as scheduled, moving us *always* (including those minutes or hours or years which seem most useless or wasted or unendurable) "toward the goal of true maturity" (Rom 12:2 JBP). Believe God. Turn the interruptions over to Him. He is at the controls.  □

## 4 *Apportioned Limitations*

THE GOD WHO DETERMINED the measurements of the foundations of the earth sets limitations to the scope of our work. It is always tempting to measure ourselves by one another, but this easily leads to boasting or despair. It is our business to find the sphere of service allotted to us, and do all that He has appointed us to do within that sphere, not "commending ourselves."

Paul said, "We will keep to the limits God has apportioned us" (2 Cor 10:13 RSV). Jesus did that—willing to become a helpless, newborn baby, to be a growing child, an adolescent, a man, each stage bounded by its peculiar strictures, yet each offering adequate scope in which to glorify his Father.

Lord, glorify yourself through me and in the place You've set me. Let me not covet another's place or work or glory.  □

## 5 *Hatred of Authority*

THE REBELLION OF KORAH took place because he and 250 "leaders of the congregation, well-known men," could not stand the distinctions God had made in the organization of his people Israel. Moses and Aaron were singled out to exercise authority; Korah and the others protested that *all* were holy, that no one should have prominence. Moses pointed out that others had been separated, brought near to the Lord, given service in the tabernacle, appointed to minister to the congregation. "And would you seek the priesthood also?" (Nm 16:10 NEB). Their so doing was diagnosed by Moses as rebellion against *God*. Hatred against authority, even any earthly authority appointed by God, is rebellion against God.

Lord, teach me to take gladly the place You have assigned to me and to submit humbly to those over me, that I may do my part to keep the smooth and proper functioning of the body of Christ.  □

# 6 *Detours*

WHEN PHARAOH LET THE PEOPLE GO, "God did not guide them by the road towards the Philistines, though that way was the shortest.... God made them go round by way of the wilderness towards the Red Sea" (Ex 13:17, 18 NEB). The direct route would save time as well as wear and tear on the people, but God had something infinitely more important than economics in mind—He wanted the people to be able to sing the song of praise of chapter 15—"The Lord is my refuge and my defence ... my deliverer. He is my God and I will glorify Him; He is my father's God and I will exalt Him" (Ex 15:2 NEB). They sang this song because they had firsthand experience of God's power and deliverance. Pursued by all the chariots and horses, cavalry and infantry of Egypt, they had passed through the Red Sea in safety and seen the enemy drowned. They would have missed this glorious lesson if they had taken the short road. When we are puzzled by delays and detours, let us think about the great purpose of life: to glorify God. The lessons He wants to teach us "in the wilderness" are priceless means of providing us with a song we could not otherwise have sung: "In Thy constant love Thou hast led the people!" (Ex 15:13).  □

# 7 The Way Appointed

ONE ASPECT OF THE MYSTERY of God's sovereign will is how the calculated evil of men is not only permitted, but actually becomes a necessary part of the divine plan. We are tempted to think of the wrongs done to us as hindrances, frustrations, interruptions. "What has *this* got to do with the will of God?" we ask, irritated and, we suppose, justifiably impatient with human interference. But the truth is that both our time and our way are in God's hands—they are "appointed." Surely it is so for all his sons as it was for the Son of Man. When He was on the verge of being "handed over for crucifixion," and betrayed by one of his own disciples, He said, "*My appointed time* is near.... One who has dipped his hand into this bowl with me will betray me. The Son of Man is going *the way appointed* for him" (Mt 26:18, 24 NEB).

Out of the deepest depths of human evil the good God brought salvation—the very salvation of man whose sinfulness killed the Son He sent.

Nothing can reach us, from any source in earth or hell, no matter how evil, which God cannot turn to his own redemptive purpose. Let us be glad that the way is not a game of chance, a mere roll of dice which determines our fortune or calamity—it is a way *appointed*, and it is appointed for God's eternal glory and our final good. □


# 8 You Can't Keep Both Eyes

A YOUNG MAN WAS DELIVERED from a life of self-destruction in the form of drug abuse. He turned from his old ways, but of course was pursued by the enemy and tempted back. It was clear to him that he could not afford to be lenient with himself in allowing the least indulgence in the old habit. One day he said to his pastor, "Don't ever allow me to use the word 'struggle.' Every time I use it I am excusing disobedience, I am really prefering to 'struggle' rather than to *quit*."

Jesus made this necessity sharply clear when He said, "If it is your eye that is your undoing, *tear it out and fling it away*; it is better to enter into life with one eye than to keep both eyes and be thrown into the fires of hell" (Mt 5:29).

To struggle—that is, to allow a "little bit" of sin, to be cautious with ourselves, tolerant of a certain amount of plain disobedience, is to try to keep both eyes.  □

# 9 Does Prayer Work?

THE ANSWER TO THAT DEPENDS on one's definition of work. It is necessary to know what a thing is for in order to judge whether it works. It would be senseless, for example, to say that if a screwdriver fails to drive nails into a board it doesn't "work." A screwdriver works very well for driving screws. Often we expect to arrange things according to our whims by praying about them, and when the arrangement fails to materialize we conclude that prayer doesn't work. God wants our willing cooperation in the bringing in of his kingdom. If "Thy kingdom come" is an honest prayer, we will seek to ask for whatever contributes to that end. What, after all is said and done, do you want above all? Is it "Thy will be done"? If so, leave it to Him.

Is it "My will be done"? Don't waste your time and God's by praying. Have it your way.  □

# 10 Clay Pots

THE JUNGLE INDIANS OF ECUADOR make clay pots of very simple design with no ornamentation or glaze. They challenged me to try shaping them as they did, rolling "snakes" of wet clay and then coiling them round and round until they had a perfectly smooth and balanced vessel. It looked rather easy, but I found that it was a highly developed skill, and my attempts to imitate it were laughable. Mine was not a master hand.

The next step was to build a very hot fire of thorns and brushwood and bake the pot. It was then ready for use, to carry water from the river or to cook in. Nobody thought much about the pot itself once it was made. What mattered was what was in it.

We are, Paul said, clay pots. The Potter has formed us, shaped us into a useful vessel, put us through the fire of testing that we might be fit to hold what He gives us. We are useful and fit—but we are still *clay pots*—it's what's inside that matters. It is a priceless treasure (2 Cor 4:7 NEB).

I can think of no clearer analogy of our place in God's service and a no more accurate picture of the *relative* merits of who we are and what we have to offer. We shall always be just *pots*, quite cheap on the market, but what we carry for others is priceless.

Love, Paul said in another passage, does not "cherish inflated ideas of its own importance" (1 Cor 13:4 JBP).  □


# 11 Confusion

THERE ARE MANY BEWILDERED and miserable Christians today. Confusion seems to characterize many Christian homes; marriages are described as "a mess"; kids are called "mixed up";

people say they can't "get their heads together." There is a clue to the cause of all this in Matthew 9:35. It is the lack of authority. When a flock of sheep is left without a shepherd, they are bewildered and miserable, not knowing what to do, where to go. No one is there to lead them.

Where there is no word of authority, there is no direction, no control, no power, for power comes by restraint and guidance. The Lord, our Shepherd, leads us to pleasant pastures and refreshing waters which are for our own good. He leads us also in paths of righteousness *for his name's sake*. Disobedience to his authority results in confusion. This disobedience to God's authority frequently shows itself in refusal to exercise or to obey the authority God has assigned here on earth, in government, work, church, and home. No wonder there is bewilderment and misery.  □

## 12 *Where God Is Taking Us*

BISHOP LESLIE NEWBIGIN, in his *South India Diary*, tells of the union of churches which took place in South India in 1947. It was the culmination of nearly fifty years of prayer and work on the part of Indians and missionaries. At the second synod a memorable sentence was spoken: "The demand to know where we are going is one which no Christian has a right to make." The bishop writes, "In a very real sense we do not know where we are going, but we are trying to meet day by day the plain requirements of God's will. This means a constant effort to bring every part of church life and practice to the test of conformity with the Gospel."

It is not for the flock of sheep to know the pasture the Shepherd has in mind. It is for them simply to follow Him. If they knew that his plans included a valley of deep shadow, they would panic. Keeping close to the one they have learned to trust is all that is necessary. He will faithfully provide rest, refreshment, correction, and protection as the needs arise. His accompanying presence is guaranteed, all the way—even through the darkest shadows—to the house of the Lord.  □

## 13  No Evidence of Progress

AT TIMES NOTHING SEEMS to be happening. So it must be for the bird that sits on her nest. Things are apparently at a standstill. But the bird sits quietly, knowing that in the stillness something vital is going on, and in the proper time it will be shown. It takes faith and patience for the bird, and such faith and patience never seem to waver, day after day, night after night, as she bides the appointed time.

Restless and doubtful we wonder why we have nothing to show for our efforts, no visible evidence of progress. Let us remember the perfect egg—unchanged in its appearance from the day it is laid. But while the bird waits faithfully, doing the only thing she is required to do throughout those silent weeks, important things are taking place.

I wait for the Lord. My soul waits,
   and in His word I hope;

my soul waits for the Lord more
   than watchmen for the morning. (Ps 130:5, 6 RSV)  □

## 14  Is Faith Easy?

A YOUNG MAN ASKED ME last night if it was easier to trust God here in this country, in this comfortable house, than it was "down where all the disasters were," meaning, I suppose, in the jungle. No, I told him, you live by faith wherever you are. The house was robbed last week—a small reminder that all that I am *and have* belongs to the Lord, to do with as He chooses. There are enough "disasters" anywhere to keep one trusting God. In the jungle there is the immanent presence of snakes, vampires, scorpions, electric eels, etc.—to say nothing of savages' spears. In Hamilton there are thieves, the possibility of fire, plumbing or electrical breakdowns, and hanging over us at all times threats of war, totalitarianism, secular humanism, economic collapse, cancer, not to mention the "small" emergencies which can bring our best-laid plans to a halt.

"I have become absolutely convinced that neither death nor life . . . neither what happens today nor what may happen tomorrow *has any power* to separate us from the love of God" (Rom 8:38-39 JBP). So wrote Paul, whose life did not represent a series of events in which we would say it was "easy to trust." It was not easy. It was *necessary.* A life free from suffering would be a life in which faith in God would be a mere frill. A human life, on the contrary, is one in which faith is a necessity. Only a fool tries to do without it.  □

## 15  *Fear God and Fear Nothing Else*

THE WORLD IS SHAKING with fear. "What will become of us? Where will it all end? What if Russia . . . ? What if cancer . . . ? What if depression . . . ?" The love of God has wrapped us round from before the foundations of the world. If we fear Him—that is, if we are brought to our knees before Him, reverence and worship Him in absolute assurance of his sovereignty, we cannot possibly be afraid of anything else. To love God is to destroy all other fear. To love the world is to be afraid of everything—what it may think of me, what it may do to me, what may happen today or tomorrow for which I am not prepared.

"The Lord is the stronghold of my life—of whom shall I be afraid?" (Ps 27:1 RSV).

And yet, Lord, the truth is that I am often afraid. I confess it. All the weight of your promises seems sometimes to be only a feather, and the weight of my fears is lead. Reverse that, Lord, I pray. Give me the healthy fear that will make light of all the others—"The fear of the Lord is life; he who is full of it will rest untouched by evil" (Prv 19:23 NEB). □

# 16 The Need for Silence

IT IS ALWAYS EASIER to add to the noise of the world than to be silent. Silence is a very precious thing—"There was silence in heaven about the space of half an hour" (Rv 8:1 AV), when the seventh seal was opened in the Book of the Revelation. Thunder and horses and martyrs and earthquakes had preceded the opening of this seal. Hail, fire, blood, and fearful judgment followed it—but in between, angels stood in the presence of God and there was utter silence. Have we learned to stand in God's presence, mouths shut, hearts open? "Lord, what do you want me to do?" We must be quiet in order to know Him and to hear Him and to hear Him answer us.

"If any of you lack wisdom let him ask his friends." No. That is not the Word of the Lord. "If any of you lack wisdom let him ask of God" (Jas 1:5 AV) is his Word to us. There is a place for asking wisdom of godly friends, but let us always go first to God.

"Be still"—that is, *shut up*—"and know that He is God" (Ps 46:10 AV). □

# 17 Stop Quivering

"THE KING'S HEART QUIVERED as the trees in the forest shake before the wind" (Is 7:2 RSV), Isaiah tells us in the story of Syria's occupation of Ephraim. The worst had happened. The thing Ahaz feared had come upon him, and he was terrified. So are we when we seem to have no defense against something. We are at the mercy of an enemy—debt or disease or disaster or doubt—and we wait, quivering in fear, for our final ruin. Then we are reminded of our sure defense, the only absolutely impregnable stronghold— the word of the Lord, and when He speaks ("This plan shall not succeed, it shall never come to pass") as He did to Ahaz, we are safe. No power on earth (or in heaven or hell) can shake the Rock of our salvation. It is on that Rock that we plant our faith and stop quivering.  □

# 18 God's Help for God's Assignment

SOMETIMES A TASK WE HAVE BEGUN takes on seemingly crushing size, and we wonder what ever gave us the notion that we could accomplish it. There is no way out, no way around it, and yet we cannot contemplate actually carrying it through. The rearing of children or the writing of a book are illustrations that come to mind. Let us recall that the task is a divinely appointed one, and divine aid is therefore to be expected. Expect it! Ask for it, wait for it, believe that God gives it. Offer to Him the job itself, along with your fears and misgivings about it. He will not fail or be discouraged. Let his courage encourage you. The day will come when the task will be finished. Trust Him for it.

"For the Lord God will help me; therefore shall I not be confounded, therefore have I set my face like a flint, and I know that I shall not be ashamed" (Is 50:7 AV).  □

# 19 A Safeguard for the Soul

SOULS ARE VULNERABLE THINGS. They need safeguards. It was when Paul was in prison that this idea came to him. He had just been writing to the Philippians about the benefits that accrued because of his own sufferings and the possible death he might die. He told them of Epaphroditus illness and anxiety, and finished with "In conclusion, my brothers, delight yourselves in the Lord!... You will find it a great safeguard to your souls" (Phil 3:1 JBP).

It would be very easy to allow depression and anxiety to overcome us when we look at the dismal circumstances in which we sometimes find ourselves. Who had better reason than Paul for depression? ("Oh well, but he was Saint Paul!" we counter.) He had learned by practice how to apply the soul's safeguard, which is not mere enjoyment. It is *delight*. This is a command and therefore an act of will, and it is done *in the Lord*. No circumstance is so dismal as to prevent obedience to the command. No trouble can blast that safeguard. Do it. Do it by faith. Delight yourself in the Lord. Maybe you will have to get out of bed, get up from your chair, go outdoors and walk, sing a song out loud, bake a pie for somebody, or mow the lawn as an offering of praise. You *can* do something which will help you to obey that command. It is amazing how strongly what we *do* affects how we *feel*.  □

# 20 The Fruit of Forgivness

EVERY DAY I AM FORGIVEN for many sins of many kinds, and although on the one hand forgiveness seems such an impossible thing (but grace is greater than all my sin), on the other hand I receive it often without wonder and nearly always without offering any "fruit."

When the Lord punished Israel, Isaiah wrote: "Only then can the fruit of his forgiveness be shown: they must smash their stone altars into pounded chalk" (Is 27:9 JBP).

When I acknowledge a specific sin, it is a good thing to do something specific to demonstrate my determination to forsake it. Smash an altar, sacrifice an hour of sleep or a meal (if the sin has been, e.g., failure to do what I want to do "because I haven't time"), write a note of apology to one sinned against, make restitution in some way for a wrong. To arise and obey in such a particular act is an appropriate sign of the genuineness of my repentance—the fruit of forgiveness.  □

## 21  Where Do We Start?

TO BE TRANSFORMED into the image of Christ I must begin to do the will of the Father in the same place where He began: He emptied Himself. There is for any serious disciple, quite simply, no other starting place. It is a matter of beginning today to say no to yourself—specifically, about something you've been insisting you must have, specifically about something you have been refusing. This is step one. You travel the road "toward Jerusalem" from there, gladly taking up the cross (which is step two: saying yes to God) and following, knowing where the road led Jesus. It did not—and don't forget this!—*end* with a cross. The third day He rose again from the dead. He ascended into heaven. His prayer for us is, "Father, I desire that these men who are thy gift to me, may be with me where I am" (Jn 17:24 NEB).  □

## 22 Difficulties Are Proof Contexts

REPEATEDLY I AM ASKED variations of this question: Did the Lord comfort you or were you sometimes lonely or sad? It is not an either-or thing. If I had not been lonely and sad at times, how could I have needed, received, or appreciated comfort? It is the sick who need the physician, the thirsty who need water. This is why Paul not only did not deplore his weaknesses, he "gloried" in them, for they provided the very occasions for his appropriating divine help and strength.

It was *in* prison that Joseph knew the presence of the Lord.

It was *in* the lion's den that Daniel's faith was proved.

It was *in* the furnace that Daniel's three friends found themselves accompanied by a fourth.

We have plenty of "proof texts"—but in order to experience their truth we have to be placed in "proof contexts." The prison, the lion's den, the furnace are where we are shown the realities, incontestably and forever. □

## 23 What Shall I Do?

IT IS NOT ALWAYS POSSIBLE to know whether the source of an idea or deed is God or Satan, since God sometimes covers Himself in cloud and Satan is often an angel of light. It is, however, always possible to trust the Shepherd who has promised to lead us in paths of righteousness. We *must* do the thing that appears to be right to do at the right time and do it by faith. That is, we do it with an honest desire to obey God and a willingness to have what He wills us to have, or not to have what He does not will us to have. If it were not for uncertainties, we would have no need to walk by faith.

Show me the way that I must take;
  to Thee I offer all my heart.
Teach me to do thy will for thou art my God.
Keep me safe, O Lord, for the honor of thy name.

(Ps 143:8, 10, 11 NEB)  □

## 24 Submission and Independence

PAUL TELLS US TO SUBMIT to one another out of reverence for
Christ, and James tells us we ought to have "the right sort of
independence" (Jas 1:4 JBP). Can the same person obey both
commands? The answer is yes, for in both he is being obedient to
Christ. Submission is the recognition of and obligation to
authority. An independence that refuses all accountability to
those assigned by God to exercise authority—parents, husbands, employers, teachers, government—is the wrong sort.
The right sort, according to James, begins with the acceptance
of adversity. That in itself indicates a measure of maturity. One
who has not attained that maturity but tries to achieve
independence will certainly have the wrong sort. To accept
adversity, obviously, goes against the grain of all of us. We don't
like adversity. Acceptance takes fortitude and faith—faith that
Somebody knows what this trouble is all about and has the
situation well in hand. In other words, acceptance is submission
to God Himself. Often the real proof of our obedience is the
willingness to submit, not only to adversity, but also to the
specific individuals whom God has put over us (and sometimes
this comes to the same thing—those individuals *spell* "adversity!"). Take a close look at what James says: whatever tests our
faith leads in the end to the right sort of independence.  □

# 25  Is It Good for Me?

YESTERDAY WE LOOKED at a piece of property on the sea. There were lovely woods to one side, two tall, scraggly, very picturesque pine trees on the other, huge rocks which turn pink in the sunset below, and in front miles and miles of blue ocean.

It is not always easy to know whether a thing we long for is a temptation from Satan to distract us from obedience and make us discontent, or something God actually wants to give us and therefore wants us to pray for. There is no such thing as something "too good to be true." God is loving and lavishly generous and has promised to give what is good—that is, what He who is omniscient knows to be good for us.

So today I asked Him to give me the prayers He wants me to pray and to give or withhold anything according to his plan for me. Nothing is too big to ask of Him, not even an ocean lot. It is God's business to decide if it is good for me. It is my business to obey Him.

"No good thing will He withhold from them that walk uprightly" (Ps 84:11 AV). □

# 26  Transforming Power

IF GOD IS ALMIGHTY, there can be no evil so great as to be beyond his power to transform. That transforming power brings light out of darkness, joy out of sorrow, gain out of loss, life out of death.

Sometimes we boggle at the evil in the world and especially in ourselves, feeling that *this* sin, *this* tragedy, *this* offense cannot possibly fit into a pattern for good. Let us remember Joseph's imprisonment, David's sin, Paul's violent persecution of Christians, Peter's denial of his Master. None of it was beyond the power of grace to redeem and turn into something productive.

The God who establishes the shoreline for the sea also decides the limits of the great mystery which is evil. He is "the Blessed Controller of all things." God will finally be God, Satan's best efforts notwithstanding. □

## 27 Will God Explain Why?

WE SOMETIMES IMAGINE that God must eventually "sit us down" and "explain" his mysterious ways to our satisfaction. Let us suppose we have never seen a skyscraper. We discover a whole city block surrounded by a board fence. Finding a knothole, we peer inside. Huge earth movers are at work; hundreds of men in hard hats are busy at mysterious tasks; cranes are being moved into place; truckloads of pipes and cement are being unloaded. What on earth is happening? There is nobody around to answer our questions. If we wait long enough, nobody will need to. When we see the finished building, all the incomprehensible activity becomes comprehensible. "Oh! So *this* is what *that* was for."

"I shall be satisfied when I awake, with Thy likeness" (Ps 17:15 AV). □

## 28 The Lord Keeps Faith

WHEN TROUBLE COMES, we are tempted to think we are being punished or that God has forgotten us. He never forgets. He keeps faith—that is He keeps his promises, is faithful to his word, even when it appears that we are forsaken.

Joseph suffered one disaster after another. When, because of the vicious lie of a rejected woman he was put in prison, the Lord was with him there, keeping faith (Gn 39:21). Perhaps Joseph wondered why Almighty God could not have prevented the woman's triumphing over him—or prevented his ever having been victimized by his brothers in the first place and thus being at this woman's mercy. But we are given the complete picture which Joseph did not have while he was in prison—the amazing purpose of God for his chosen people, Jacob and all his family, who because of Joseph's long-drawn-out sufferings, were saved. God keeps faith—He has a perfect blueprint, and He is building according to its specifications.  □

## 29 *Gentle as a Nurse*

A GOOD NURSE DOES NOT PAMPER her charge, but seeks his best interest with fortitude, consistency, and love. Paul's love for the new Christians at Thessalonica was like that. It was no sentimental feeling. He writes of having brought them the Word:

in the power of the Holy Spirit, and with strong conviction.
(1 Thes 1:5)

frankly and fearlessly, by the help of our God. A hard struggle it was. (1 Thes 2:2)

We do not curry favor with men. Our words have never been flattering words ... or a cloak for greed. (1 Thes 2:4, 5)

We have never sought honor from men, from you or anyone else. ... We were as gentle with you as a nurse caring fondly for her children. (1 Thes 2:6, 7)

Here is the pattern for all who would do God's work with souls: faithful giving of the Word, a heart true and pure in seeking God's glory, gentleness, self-giving, and plain hard work.  □

# 30 Content to Be Weak

WHAT WEAKNESS ARE YOU FEELING today? The inability to manage circumstances that cry out to be changed? Helplessness in the face of another's deep need, or of evil you have to watch perpetrated on others you love? A sense of inadequacy for some task laid upon you? Physical weakness or pain? The need for power to forgive an injury or keep silence about unjust accusations against you?

Christ has been there before you. Every form of human limitation He knew, and out of that utter *poverty* we have been made strong. Yet, again and again, in the life of each disciple, comes the experience of weakness in order that we may live his life for others.

"We who share His weakness shall by the power of God live with Him in your service" (2 Cor 13:4 NEB).

This sharing of his weakness is one aspect of the death of the cross, one of the conditions of our discipleship, and hence cause for joy rather than bitterness. For we walk the road, not alone, but with Christ, "well content to be weak at any time if only you are strong" (2 Cor 13:9 NEB). The mystery is constantly being worked out—strength out of weakness, life out of death. □

# 31 The Terms

"THE MAN WHO IS CHALLENGED by Fate does not take umbrage at the terms," wrote Dag Hammarskjold. So the man called by Christ. Any terms at all are acceptable if we may be permitted to walk with Him.

"But is *this* the path, Lord? Must we take *this* one in order to reach Home?"

"Trust Me."

When the way to the house of the Lord leads through the "Valley of the Shadow," we accept those terms, too. If we suffer loss, scorn, misunderstanding, false accusation, or any other form of trouble, it is what we agreed on to begin with. Compared with the rewards promised, it is nothing; so let us not take umbrage. Let us be quite clear and matter-of-fact about it: "In the world you have tribulation; but be of good cheer [*cheer up!*] I have overcome the world" (Jn 16:33). □

## MONTH FOUR

### *1 His or Ours?*

THE PROPERTY ON THE SEA is now ours. We can hardly believe it.

"But it was what you had dreamed of, wasn't it?"

"Yes, Lord."

"Did I not promise long ago to give you the desires of your heart? This is one of them. Often I cannot give them in the form you dream of because it would not, in the end, give you happiness. This time I give exactly what you asked. What will you do with it now?"

"First we thank you, Lord. Then we offer it back to You. Do with it, for us, for anyone who comes here, as You choose. Make it a place of peace, a desired haven."

"I receive your offering. Whose is it now?"

"Yours, Lord. Help me to remember this as King David remembered it when he prayed, 'Everything comes from thee, and it is only of thy gifts that we give to thee. We are aliens before thee and settlers ... everything is thine'" (1 Chr 29:14, 15, 16 NEB). □

# 2 *An Encircling Shield*

DIFFERENT PHASES OF LIFE have different sets of fears. A newborn baby demonstrates fear of falling and of loud noises. Swaddling clothes, used for thousands of years, are still wound tightly around the babies of the Quichua Indian tribe of Ecuador. As soon as a child is born his arms are bound to his sides, his legs straightened in a neat firm package. When this is removed the baby feels insecure and cries.

Adolescent fears about popularity, pimples, and peer pressure give way to adult anxieties about responsibility and life's major decisions.

As we grow old we are beset by the fear of aging, which may bring us weakness, pain, dependence on others, loneliness. We wake in the early dark and find ourselves the targets of many fiery darts of fear. We may think we are on guard, and suddenly a dart comes at us from an unexpected angle. We can't cover all the possibilities. We dodge and duck, but some of the fears get to us—unless we take refuge in the Lord. The psalmist calls Him "my encircling shield, my glory." No need to stare into the darkness, allowing our imaginations to torment us with the "what ifs"—"Now I can lie down and go to sleep and then awake, for the Lord has hold of me" (Ps 3:3, 5 JB).  □

# 3 *Thy List Be Done*

I AM A LIST-MAKER. Every day I make a list of what I must do. I have an engagement calendar and an engagement book. I have a grocery list on the wall beside the refrigerator, last year's Christmas list in this year's engagement book (so I won't duplicate gifts), a master list for packing my suitcase (so I won't forget anything), a prayer list (a daily one and a special one for each day of the week), and several others.

Recently a wholly unexpected minor operation badly interrupted my list of things to be done that week. But because God is my sovereign Lord, I was not worried. He manages perfectly, day and night, year in and year out, the movements of the stars, the wheeling of the planets, the staggering coordination of events that goes on on the molecular level in order to hold things together. There is no doubt that He can manage the timing of my days and weeks. So I can pray in confidence, *Thy list, not mine,* be done.  ☐

## 4 *Spiritual Equilibrium*

SOMETIMES A HOPE OR DESIRE lays hold on one with such power that it becomes almost burdensome, even though the thing is a delight to contemplate. The ordinary business of life must be attended to, but this thing carries a lot of weight in soul, mind, and heart. It has a strong pull. And when you are carrying a heavy weight, you have to compensate in order to keep your balance. The best means to spiritual equilibrium, I find, is to look repeatedly at the things which are not seen, that is, at things which are eternal. What Evelyn Underhill calls "the pressure of the Divine Charity" forever urges me forward, counteracting the pressure of my emotions and human desires, reminding me with great patience and great persistence that this thing—this love, this longing, this huge desire—is the very thing God Himself gave, in order that I might have "somewhat to offer." He will see to it that it does not come to *nothing,* provided we lay it before Him, put it at his disposal.

Lord, all that I long for is known to you,
my sighing is no secret from you ...
I put my trust in you, Yahweh,
and leave you to answer for me, Lord my God.
(Ps 38:9, 15 JB)  ☐

# 5 Able to Receive

A YOUNG WOMAN ASKED recently why it is that godly professors in her seminary are on opposite sides of certain doctrinal fences. A partial answer is that we know only in part. None of us sees the whole truth, and what we do see is "through a glass darkly." We are at different stages of the journey. Sometimes I sympathize with the author of Psalm 119—"Gusts of anger seize me as I think of evil men who forsake Thy law"—and wish I could force people to accept what I see as truth. Jesus did not force them. "With many such parables He would give them His message, *so far as they were able to receive it*" (Mk 4:33 NEB). There may be some who are willing but not able to receive, others able but not willing. Only God can be sure who's who. We are to be faithful in transmitting the message and willing to respect the hearer. If God grants him freedom of will to receive or reject, so must I. If he is as yet unable to receive it, I must entrust him to God, remembering the narrow limits of my own understanding as well.  □

# 6 Sunrise Is an Act of God

THE NIGHT SKY, when I went to the front window this morning, was a clear dark blue, with a few sharp stars. Now, as it reddens toward dawn, a thick quilt of slate-colored cloud is moving over the whole sky, leaving only a strip of rose gold. But I am sure the sun will rise even though covered with a quilt.

We assume the sun will always rise. It always has. But it rises because God continues to will it so, not because it must in and of itself. I breathe, not because I am a smoothly functioning breathing machine, but because He who holds my breath in his hand wills me to breathe, as He wills the squirrel to breathe in the oak grove beside my house and the crow that perches in the scrub pine.

The will of God is not a given quantity. It is creative, dynamic, flowing action. Jesus participated in that action by submitting to the Will and moving with power along the "appointed way," according to the "appointed time," choosing the Father's will above his own.

The sun does no choosing. God chooses—every morning so far—to make it rise. Yet the Lord of the universe asks me to choose to follow Him—to participate, as Christ did, in the flowing action which is his will. "Dwell in my love. If you heed my commands, you will dwell in my love, as I have heeded my Father's commands and dwell in His love" (Jn 15:10 NEB).  □

# 7 Time for God

IT IS A GOOD AND NECESSARY thing to set aside time for God in each day. The busier the day, the more indispensable is this quiet period for prayer, Bible reading, and silent listening. It often happens, however, that I find my mind so full of earthly matters that it seems I have gotten up early in vain and have wasted three-fourths of the time so dearly bought (I do love my sleep!). But I have come to believe that the act of will required to arrange time for God may be an offering to Him. As such He accepts it, and what would otherwise be "loss" to me I count as "gain" for Christ. Let us not be "weary in well-doing," or discouraged in the pursuit of holiness. Let us, like Moses, go to the Rock of Horeb—and God says to us what He said to him, "You will find me waiting for you there" (Ex 17:6 NEB).  □

# 8 Iron Shoes

WHEN SOME OUT—OF—THE ORDINARY supply is needed in order for us to accomplish the job given, we can be confident it will be provided. "Shoes of iron" were asked in Moses' blessing for Asher, an impossibly long-lasting provision from God. The old spiritual says, "I got shoes, you got shoes, all God's children got shoes," but not all God's children have iron ones; only those who need them. Our heavenly Father knows exactly what we will require to fulfill his purposes for us. It is wrong—it is, in fact, a sin—for us to worry about where the "shoes" will come from. "Trust me!" God says to us. "I'll give you iron ones if only iron ones can do the job."

I worried this morning about the seeming impossibility of doing everything that needs to be done before Wednesday when we are moving to a new house. Then I remembered that strength according to my day's need is promised in the same verse (Dt 33:25), and any special need—"iron shoes" or whatever—will also be forthcoming. □

# 9 A Faith Untried

"A FAITH UNTRIED is no faith at all," someone has said. Today I declared my faith before a hundred women and came home to a startling piece of bad news. Hopes were dashed, plans ruined, over a seemingly trivial thing. We did not know what to do. "Trust me" is always the word at such a time. "But Lord, we *did* trust You. You answered us and everything was working so beautifully. Now this. What shall we do?" "Keep on trusting me. That is my assignment for you tonight. Commit your way to Me; trust in Me; stand still and see."

Why, of course, Lord! I see what You mean. How could I be

sure I'm trusting You unless You keep giving me "pop quizzes"? These are the exams in the school of faith.

"More precious than perishable gold is faith which has stood the test. These trials come so that your faith may prove itself worthy" (1 Pt 1:7 NEB).  □

## 10 Constructive Love

TODAY WILL BE FULL OF TURMOIL, for we are moving. Decisions to be made, complicated sorting and packing to be done, hard physical work, confusion and misunderstanding. I will be tempted to "manage" things which are not mine to manage, to be impatient and anxious and vindictive—I can see it coming! But there is a quiet, steadying power—the love of Christ, and "this love of which I speak is slow to lose patience, looks for a way of being constructive" (1 Cor 13:4 JBP). It is not in me. That brand of love is not a part of my nature. So I simply ask for it. Lord, your love alone, at work in me, behaves like that.

> Love through me, Love of God.
> Make me like thy clear air
> Through which, unhindered, colors pass
> As if it were not there.
> (Amy Carmichael, Toward Jerusalem)  □

## 11 The Fact of the Resurrection

A METROPOLITAN (bishop) of the Orthodox Church in Russia was faced with an atheist in the congregation who loudly declared, "Today nobody believes in the resurrection of Christ." Instead of answering the claim, the metropolitan cried out, "Christ is risen!" and the hall, which was supposedly filled with atheists, responded with a roar, "Indeed He is risen!"

This is the proclamation of faith. It is often a waste of time and energy to argue with doubters—including ourselves. If we are assailed with unbelief, let us return to the bedrock of faith: the resurrection, for without this our faith is certainly vain. Let us shout (even alone with our private doubts) *Christ is risen!* It is a fact. Everything else is trivial by comparison. ☐

## 12 *The Power of Darkness*

WHEN THE CHIEF PRIESTS, Temple officers, and elders came to the Garden of Gethsemane to arrest Jesus, they succeeded only because a sovereign God permitted them to succeed. Jesus pointed out that He was teaching daily in the Temple, yet they never laid a finger on Him. Now they were after Him with swords and staves. "But this is your hour, and the power of darkness is yours" (Lk 22:53 JBP). Who gave them that hour? Who allowed them the power to capture Him? It was God, without whose leave not even a sparrow can fall to the ground. God is omnipotent, never slumbering, just, righteous, and forever in control. He was not taken by surprise. All was working then, as it is always working, into a pattern for good.

Our own difficulties often appear to be random. Our tragedies look wildly uncontrolled. They are not. They are *subject.* Limits are set. God is quietly at work, standing in the shadows, ceaselessly watching over His children.

"The light shines on in the dark, and the darkness has never mastered it" (Jn 1:5 NEB). ☐

# 13 Responsibility

AN IMPORTANT SIGN of maturity is the acceptance of responsibility. One quits depending on everybody else and acknowledges that certain duties are his alone. If he doesn't do them, nobody will. Every day there is, for example, a "cross" to take up. Who else is going to carry it? It is mine. It lies in my pathway, and unless I accept it—and accept it gladly for Christ—I simply am not following Him. He has made it perfectly clear that there are two prerequisites to following, that is, to being his disciple: denying oneself, and taking up one's cross. To know yourself is to know your cross. Francois Mauriac says, "to flee one's sorrow and evade and ignore one's cross is the whole occupation of the world; but that occupation is at the same time a fleeing from one's own self"—or, we may say, from our proper and assigned responsibility. We may not always see a particular task laid before us, but one thing is sure: to trust Him *is* a task, proper to every Christian, assigned to us every minute of every hour of every day, and to flee this task is worldly, irresponsible, and immature.

"The Lord is my light and my salvation. Whom shall I fear?" (Ps 27:1 AV).

"*I will trust*, and not be afraid" (Is 12:2 AV). □

# 14 Not to Be Served but to Serve

IT IS THE MARK of a mature man that his sense of responsibility takes precedence over his own feelings. It is a mark of godliness that he acknowledges God's care of all men, not only of himself. Moses was such a man. When God told him that he must go up Mt. Nebo, look over the land promised to Israel, and then die without entering into it because of his disobedience at Meribah, there is not a word of resentment of self-pity or self-justification from Moses. Instead his concern was for the people he had been shepherding, that they might be "brought home." The God to whom he addressed the prayer was "God of the spirits of all mankind." Moses saw things with a vision that encompassed far more than his own horizon.

Lord, deliver us from smallness and self-pity. "Make us masters of ourselves that we may be the servants of others"(Sir Alexander Patterson). □

# 15 A Strange Godsend

KING SAUL WAS TORMENTED in a strange way from time to time by an evil spirit from God (1 Sm 16:14). His servants suggested that harp music might drive it away. One of them told the king about Jesse's son David of Bethlehem who could play, and who was also a brave man, a good fighter, wise in speech, and handsome. Furthermore, the Lord was with him. David was sent for, and besides these God-given gifts, he brought with him a homer of bread, a skin of wine, and a kid. The king loved him and made him his armor-bearer. Whenever the evil spirit came upon Saul, David would take his harp and play so that Saul found relief, recovered, and the spirit left him alone.

This story shows us that among the baffling intricacies of the sovereign plan of God there is often evil which is not only permitted but sometimes actually sent by God. We wonder why. Surely part of the reason is that we may learn our own helplessness and need of Him. Saul was a powerful king, but it took his servants, who happened to know of a small-town boy, to suggest a remedy for the king's trouble. God sent the trouble. God sent the boy. That boy had been prepared by God, equipped with gifts which the king needed. Picture the boy, idly strumming his lyre as he passed the time of day in the pasture with the sheep. He could not have dreamed of the use God would some day make of that skill—to comfort a king's tormented spirit and later to become the "sweet singer of Israel."

Lord, I believe. Help my unbelief. Give me a trust big enough to embrace the baffling intricacies and to find in times of helplessness that You are a very present Help. □

# 16 Choose to Be Glad

THE BIBLE IS FULL of commands to be joyful. The Lord commanded the people of Israel to set aside certain days for celebration, and on those days they were to rejoice. There was no provision made for any who might not happen to "feel like" rejoicing. This was what they were to do, young and old, slaves and free, aliens, orphans, and widows—in obedience to the command. The pilgrim-feast of Weeks was celebrated seven weeks after the time "when the sickle is put to the standing corn." The people were commanded to bring a freewill offering and to *rejoice.* "You shall rejoice in the place which the Lord your God shall choose. . . . you shall rejoice in your feast. . . . you shall keep the feast with joy" (Dt 16:14-15 NEB).

The rhythm of life is one of God's mercies, meant to keep us from sinking into individual ruts. We are called away from our personal inclination by the dawning of each new day, by the sun's going down so that we may cease from our work, by the changing seasons which require changes of habit, work, and dress, and by the regular occurrence of "feasts" when, without reference to how we happen to feel, we may join with others in purposeful rejoicing. We may choose to be glad.

"Although the fig-tree does not burgeon, the vines bear no fruit, the olive crop fails . . . and there are not cattle in the stalls, yet I will exult in the Lord and rejoice in the God of my deliverance" (Hb 3:17, 18 NEB). □

# 17 An Antidote for Pride

THE BASIS OF ALL SIN of whatever kind is pride. This was what inspired the disobedience of Adam and Eve, and it is always with us. One very common form it takes is the pride of privilege. When a man is given a special position, he forgets that it was *given*. He becomes proud, as though "his own arm" had gotten him the victory. God knows well the heart and made provision for this sin of pride when He instructed the Israelites about appointing a king. He was to make a copy of the law. This would be the antidote, necessary for him and likewise for all of us (for "law" read "Word"). "He shall keep it by him and read from it all his life, so that he may learn to fear the Lord his God and keep all the words of this law and observe these statutes. In this way he shall not become prouder than his fellow countrymen nor shall he turn from these commandments to right or left" (Dt 17:19, 20 NEB). The attempt itself to keep the commandments, one by one and day after day, will be sufficient to humble us, for the "straightedge of the law" (Rom 3:20 JBP) will only show us, as Paul found, how crooked we are. We will find, in fact, that we cannot keep it. "The whole matter is on a different plane—believing instead of achieving" (Rom 3:27 JBP). Pride won't find much foothold on that plane.

"The real test of being in the presence of God is that you either forget about yourself altogether or see yourself as a small, dirty object. It is better to forget about yourself altogether" (C.S. Lewis, *Mere Christianity*).  □

# 18 Where There Is Injury

HAVE YOU EVER FOUND the taste of revenge sweet? Does there lurk in your heart, as in mine at times, a desire for at least the milder forms of revenge if you have been hurt—a desire to see the person apologize, an urge to remind him that he was nasty to you, or even the temptation to pay him back somehow? It was not God's plan that man should take revenge. That He has reserved for Himself, and when we seize that power we are taking a huge risk. It is, in another form, the risk Adam and Eve took when they ate the forbidden fruit—arrogating to themselves powers, lethal burdens, for which they were never designed.

What if God paid us for our sins? What if He were not Love? His mercy is everlasting and has brought us salvation and forgiveness. Remembering that, and how we ourselves have offended Him times without number, shall we dare to retaliate when someone sins against us? Think of the measure of forgiveness God has offered us. Think of the price. Think what the cross means. Then pray the prayer of St. Francis:

Lord, make me an instrument of Thy peace—
Where there is hatred, let me sow love;
Where there is injury, pardon. . . .
For it is in forgiving that we are forgiven,
It is in dying that we are born again to eternal life.  □

# 19 Satans' Opposition or God's Punishment?

SOMETIMES WHEN WE ARE IN TROUBLE we are not sure whether the trouble is the opposition of our enemy Satan or a punishment from God. It may be both, and in any case the thing to do is pray—first, confession of sin which is known; second, asking to be shown sin which has not been acknowledged; third, prayer for deliverance in God's way and in God's time.

When the people of Israel were in great trouble and disgrace and the wall of Jerusalem had been broken down, Nehemiah sat down and wept. Then he mourned and fasted and prayed "for some days" before the God of heaven. The exile of the people and the destruction of the wall were surely the work of evil men, but they were also the means employed by a sovereign God to punish the people. *"If you are unfaithful I will scatter you."* Nehemiah reminded God in his prayer of this threat, but he also reminded Him of his promise: *"If you return and obey . . . I will gather them"* (Neh 1:8, 9 RSV). Nehemiah became the intercessor and the means in the hand of God for their restoration, just as their enemies had, under his sovereignty, been the means of their punishment.

It is not required that we sort out all the possibilities—"Is this God?" or "Is this Satan?"—it is required that we confess our sins and put our whole trust in the God who is in charge. □

## 20 Signs Do Not Nourish

IT IS THE ENEMY who tempts us, as he tempted Jesus, to demand always some *visible proof* of the miracle-working power of God: "Tell these stones to become bread" (Mt 4:3 NEB). A miracle would validate our own claim to be in close touch with the Father. But the important thing in life is not to be vindicated, nor to see miracles, but to walk by faith—that is, to take God at his word. So shall we *live.* So shall we follow Christ, content to do without the startling, the dramatic evidences that God is God, believing instead—in the face of all the enemy's taunts— the spoken Word of Him who calls Himself the I AM. Even in the wilderness, even in our isolation and hunger, we need not ask for more than the Bread of Heaven.

Give us this day, Lord,
Not the miracles our human hearts long for,
Not the proud but brief satisfaction of saying to doubters, "I told you so!"
But give us daily bread—only that which You see will truly nourish us in our pilgrimage towards home. □

# 21 Why Guidance Is Not Given

SOMETIMES WE ARE PERPLEXED because guidance does not come when we ask for it.

Some of the elders of Israel came to consult the Lord and were sitting with the prophet Ezekiel. The word of the Lord through him was, "As I live, I will not be consulted by you" (Ez 20:3 NEB). Then followed a long account of Israel's deliberate disobedience: idolatry, desecration of the Sabbath, human sacrifice, revolt, rebellion, and trespassing all God's laws.

"You are still defiling yourselves . . . how can I let you consult me?" (Ez 20:31). Only the pure in heart—those who desire nothing but the will of God—can expect his counsel and guidance.

> Create in me a clean heart, O God,
>   and renew a right spirit within me (Ps 51:10 AV).

To pray that prayer is to accept the obligation to be obedient in all that is known of God's will.  □


# 22 As Soon As You Begin to Pray

PRAYER SETS SPIRITUAL FORCES in motion, although the effect is often invisible, perhaps for a long time.

In the first year of the reign of Darius, Daniel was reading and reflecting about the seventy years of Jerusalem's lying in ruins. He turned to God in "earnest prayer and supplication with fasting and sackcloth and ashes," confessing Israel's sins and beseeching God for forgiveness and restoration. The angel Gabriel came close to him in the hour of evening sacrifice, "flying swiftly."

"As you were beginning your supplications a word went forth" (Dn 9:23 NEB), he said. The answer was already beginning to be processed when the prayer was offered. It took a very long time. Periods of weeks and years for the nation, and times of mourning, solitude, weakness, and fear on Daniel's part were required before the answer could come to pass.

We should take heart from Gabriel's message. Though our prayers seem feeble and sometimes appear to have gone unheard, a word has gone forth. Spiritual agents from the throne room of the King of kings are mobilized against spiritual forces from the headquarters of evil, and there will be ultimate victory.

"Tremendous power is made available through a good man's earnest prayer" (Jas 5:16 JBP). □

# 23 Distractions to Prayer

No one who has tried to pray for more than a few seconds at a time would claim that he is never distracted. It is astonishing to note how insistently and immediately irrelevant matters come to mind, noises occur, things to be attended to are remembered, people interrupt, and even physical discomforts or pains bother us which we had not noticed until we tried to pray. These things are, of course, the work of the master saboteur of souls, who knows how to render our spiritual machinery useless, by the loosening of the tiniest screw or the loss of the smallest nut.

Distractions can be useful. They provide constant reminders of our human weakness. We recognize in them how earthbound we are, and then how completely we must depend on the help of the Holy Spirit to pray in and through us. We are shown, by a thousand trivialities, how trivial are our concerns. The very effort to focus, even for a minute, on higher things, is foiled, and we see that prayer—the prerequisite for doing anything for God—cannot be done without Him. We are not, however, left to fend for ourselves.

"The Spirit too comes to help us in our weakness. For when we cannot choose words in order to pray properly, the Spirit himself expresses our plea in a way that could never be put into words, and God who knows everything in our hearts knows perfectly well what he means, and that the pleas of the saints expressed by the Spirit are according to the mind of God" (Rom 8:26, 27 JB). □

## 24 Running the Course

TODAY THERE ARE JUST too many things to do. My natural response is to fret and fear. Both are forbidden: Fret not. Fear not. That tells me what not to do. What, then, should I do?

"I will run the course set out in thy commandments, for they gladden my heart" (Ps 119:32 NEB).

There will be both time and strength today to run *that* course, for it is always possible to do the will of God. The course He sets for us in his commandments is not an obstacle course, but one carefully planned to suit our qualifications—that is, not too rigorous for our limitations, not too lenient for our strengths.

The plan of God for me, for this one day, is meant not to trouble but to *gladden* my heart. Christ's yoke, according to his own promise, is not hard but easy—if we bear it together with Him and if we bear it as Christ bore it, in meekness and lowliness of heart.

"We must run with resolution the race for which we are entered, our eyes fixed on Jesus, on whom faith depends from start to finish" (Heb 12:2 NEB). □

# 25 Zero Faith

"I HAD ZERO FAITH," a young woman said to me yesterday. "I believed in nothing at all. I wished I could, but it just wasn't there. I began praying, without faith, that God would help me to believe. He did. I *know* He answers that kind of prayer."

This young woman is a conscientious wife and mother, a faithful church member, and a growing Christian. Her life witnesses to the answer to her prayer. She started with nothing.

Sometimes we start with a small measure of faith, like that of the distraught father who asked Jesus for the healing of his son. "I have faith," he said, then, aware that it was not enough to support the weight of the thing he was asking, "Help me where faith falls short" (Mk 9:24 NEB).

Unbelief is a stronghold of such spiritual power that only mighty spiritual weapons can storm it. We have those weapons— "not merely human, but divinely potent to demolish strongholds" (2 Cor 10:4 NEB). Prayer is one of them. Must we be experts in its use? The young woman's testimony shows that we need not. We must only come, aware that our faith is not enough, aware that the Lord Himself waits to help us if only we ask.

Satan trembles when he sees
The weakest saint upon his knees.  □


# 26 It Is Hard to Enter

THE KINGDOM OF GOD stands over against all other "kingdoms"— that is, against all other authorities, sources of power, objects of trust. It is *hard* to enter the kingdom of God—not because an angel is set to keep us out, not because God would surround Himself with a highly selected elite, but because the condition for admittance is renunciation of all other kingdoms.

The wealthy stranger who ran up to Jesus, knelt, and inquired how he might receive eternal life "went away with a heavy heart" (Mk 10:22 NEB). He did not want to pay the price of entrance—a shift in the source of his trust, from money (which seemed concrete and dependable) to this "Good Master" who asked everything visible and dependable in exchange for what was invisible and seemingly very undependable.

Every day we are asked which kingdom we choose. Is it, in the last analysis, "thine" or "mine" which I most desire? What is it that my most earnest prayers are directed toward?  □

## 27 *What Can I Do for God?*

MOST OF US WOULD LIKE to do something "special" in life, something to distinguish us. We suppose that we desire it for God's sake, but more likely we are discontent with ordinary life and crave special privileges. When Israel asked if they should offer some spectacular sacrifice—thousands of rams, ten thousand "rivers of oil," a firstborn child—the answer was, "He has showed you, O man, what is good; and what does the Lord require of you but to do justice, and to love kindness, and to walk humbly with your God" (Mi 6:8 RSV).

There is nothing conspicuous about those requirements. It is not a "special" service for which one would be likely to be decorated or even particularly remembered. But it is worth more to God than any sacrifice.

Lord, deliver me from the delusion of imagining that my desire is to serve You, when my real desire is the distinction of serving in some way which others admire.  □

# 28 Seed and Yeast

WHEN WE SEE THINGS we believe need to be changed, most of us are impatient to see them done at once. The kingdom of God does not operate spectacularly, with a sudden rush of irresistible force, but rather like seed and yeast. These are small and wholly unimpressive and go to work only when buried. They need an appropriate medium in which to generate change, but the life-principle is there, latent but powerful, ready to begin the slow and marvelous process of transformation.

Our prayers for change—in people, in situations—are summed up in the old petition, "Thy *kingdom* come"—but when we ask for that we are asking for what may seem an excruciatingly drawn-out business. We will need the patience of the farmer and the baker who, having done the one thing needful, then quietly (and with calm faith) wait for the thing to happen.  ☐

# 29 The Answer Is Always Enough

WE OFTEN HOPE TO BE SPARED trouble or suffering, and surely it is legitimate to pray that we may be ("Lead us not into temptation" is a prayer Jesus *taught* us to pray). Jesus Himself asked the Father to take away the "cup"; Paul prayed for the removal of his "thorn." In both cases, the answer was no. But God did not give a *mere* no—He sent what had not been asked: strength to endure. An angel was immediately dispatched to Gethsemane, "bringing him strength" (Lk 22:43 NEB). His suffering did not cease—in fact, "in anguish of spirit He prayed the more urgently and his sweat was like clots of blood" (Lk 22:44).

The apostle was suffering in some physical way, it seems. The thing was called "a messenger of Satan," and he did well to ask for its removal. The answer was no—but something unasked was given: grace. There was plenteous grace to enable Paul to endure. What God gives in answer to our prayers will always be the thing we most urgently need, and it will always be sufficient.  □

## 30 Responsible to Praise

WE CANNOT ALWAYS or even often control events, but we can control how we respond to them. When things happen which dismay or appal, we ought to look to God for his meaning, remembering that He is not taken by surprise nor can his purposes be thwarted in the end. What God looks for is those who will *worship* Him. Our look of inquiring trust glorifies Him.

One of the witnesses to the crucifixion was a military officer to whom the scene was surely not a novelty. He had seen plenty of criminals nailed up. But the response of this Man who hung there was of such an utterly different nature than that of the others that the centurion knew at once that He was innocent. His own response then, rather than one of despair that such a terrible injustice should take place, or of anger at God who might have prevented it, was *praise* (Lk 23:47 NEB).

This is our first responsibility: to glorify God. In the face of life's worst reversals and tragedies, the response of a faithful Christian is praise—not *for* the wrong itself certainly, but for who God is and for the ultimate assurance that there is a pattern being worked out for those who love Him.  □

## 31 Forsaken? Impossible

TWICE IN MY LIFE I have heard Christians claim, in all seriousness, that God had forsaken them. This is an impossibility. Does Christ live in us? He does. The living Christ dwells in the heart of every true believer—He in them and they in Him. There are no words which adequately describe the intimacy of this relationship. Jesus, in his last recorded prayer for those whom the Father had given Him, asked "that they may be one, as we are one, I in them and thou in me ... that the love thou hadst for me may be in them, and I may be in them" (Jn 17:23, 26 NEB).

Jesus Christ, in the extremity of his agony on the cross, asked why God had forsaken Him. In becoming sin for us He experienced a terrible alienation from his Father, a sense of total dereliction. God did not and could not forsake the Son who was one with Him. He cannot and will not forsake us who are not only his sons and daughters, but also the dwelling-places of his only begotten Son. "'I will never, never, never, never, never (the Greek has five negatives) leave you or forsake you,'" is his promise. At times we may be overcome with a feeling of helpless forsakenness. This is surely not from the loving Father, but from the father of lies. The best way to answer that "father" is the way Jesus answered when tempted by Satan: *"It is written."* Take God's own promise with its five negatives and hold on.  □

## MONTH FIVE

# 1 *Message to the Thirsty*

WHEN JESUS WENT UP to the Feast of Tabernacles in Jerusalem, there were fierce arguments among the Jews as to his identity and his authority for speaking. He answered them, yet they refused to accept the reply and wanted only to be rid of Him. On the last day of the festival He turned to another group of whom nearly every crowd, even the most hostile, will usually contain a few—those who are thirsty for God.

"If anyone is thirsty, let him come to me" (Jn 7:37 NEB). Jesus raised his voice to issue this invitation. He wanted it to be heard above all the din of bustling and contention. Someone would be there to whom it would be like cold water. "Whoever believes in Me, let him drink."

Sometimes we are famished—confused, dry, upset by arguments and conflicting interpretations. To us the Savior says, "*Come.*" If, without the solution to all our problems, we are willing simply to believe, He says , "*Drink.*"  □

## 2 Hour of Glory

THE MIRACLE OF LAZARUS being raised from the grave brought the crowds waving palms to Jesus, proclaiming Him King. Even foreigners (some Greeks) heard of Him and asked his disciple Philip if they might see Him. This, surely, was his hour of glory.

Heaven's definition of glory, however, is a very different thing from earth's. "The hour has come," Jesus said to Philip and Andrew, "for the Son of Man to be glorified" (Jn 12:23 NEB). Then He illustrated his meaning: a grain of wheat is merely a solitary grain until it dies. It is *death* that brings glory, the glory of the rich harvest. It was not popular acclaim but popular rejection and his own suffering and death that constituted his "hour of glory," and He prayed to be spared that hour.

The one who would serve Him must understand the conditions. He must *follow*—into death—that is, he must "lose himself." Then, the promise is that he will be "kept safe for eternal life" (Jn 12:25) and *honored* by the Father. The hour of glory *is* the hour of suffering—seen from heaven's side.

Lord, be near us in our pain and grant us the clear eye of faith to see it from heaven's perspective. Jesus walked this road. Help us to follow him gladly.  □

## 3 This Love among You

"AS I HAVE LOVED YOU, so you are to love one another. If there is this love among you, then all will know that you are my disciples" (Jn 13:34, 35 NEB).

The love of Jesus for his disciples was unsentimental. As a man, He fully entered into their experience of being men, with all the feelings that entails, yet his love for them was not a feeling. It was decisive, both as attitude and act. He honored their dignity as men by treating them with trust, speaking honestly and straightforwardly, never "tiptoeing" to spare their weaker feelings, never dissimulating. At times He hurt them in order to save them. There was no care for Himself in that kind of love. He had the courage to face their anger and misunderstanding.

"If there is *this love* among you . . ." what a difference it will make in the world!  □

# 4 *All a Mistake?*

IT IS EASY TO CONCLUDE, when things turn out badly, that it was all a mistake to begin with.

The facts of the gospel do not bear this out. Think of Jesus' choice of apostles. He spent a whole night in prayer before He made his selection. Judas was one of his choices. Peter affirmed, in his sermon on the day of Pentecost, "He was one of our number and had his place in this ministry" (Acts 1:17 NEB). Things could not have turned out worse for him or for Jesus because of him, yet Scripture nowhere suggests that the original choice was a mistake. Judas was still a man, still free to sin.

When we must make decisions, we should bring to bear on them scriptural principles, prayer, and all the intelligence God has dealt out to us. Then we must go on quietly in faith, knowing that the results of our obedience are God's responsibility, not ours.  □

# 5 Enable Thy Servants

MANY OF OUR PRAYERS are for a quick and easy solution. God is more glorified in his people when they exhibit his grace under pressure. When Peter and John had been discharged by the rulers, elders, and doctors of the Jewish law with orders not to speak again in the name of Jesus, the Christians prayed about it—"They raised their voices as one man and called upon God." Their prayer was not, "Make these people stop persecuting Thy servant," but, remembering the word of prophecy concerning how the Messiah was to be treated, they asked God only to *notice* what was happening to his servants and to *enable* them to speak with boldness (Acts 4:29 NEB).

We, too, may bring any difficult situation to our heavenly Father, laying it before his eyes, and asking not for instant escape but for "enablement"—for strength to sustain the burden and do what we ought to do without the fear of man.   □

# 6 Willed Blindness

IN PAPHOS THERE LIVED a sorcerer named Elymas, who posed as a prophet. He belonged to the governor's retinue. Seized with jealousy because the governor wanted to hear the word of the Lord from Paul and Barnabas, Elymas tried to turn him aside from faith. Having seen the light, Elymas preferred darkness and preferred also that others remain in darkness if their turning to the light should turn them away from him. He thus willfully *falsified* the truth and was struck blind.

The result of deliberate deception is blindness. The man who, to preserve his own position, deceives himself or another, is a *swindler* (this is what Paul called Elymas), "rascal, son of the devil, enemy of all goodness" (Acts 13:10 NEB).

God is light, and in Him is not any darkness at all.

If we guard some corner of darkness in ourselves, we will soon be drawing someone else into darkness, shutting them out from the light in the face of Jesus Christ.

"Lighten our darkness, we beseech thee, O Lord; and by thy great mercy defend us from all perils and dangers of this night; for the love of thy only Son, our Savior, Jesus Christ. Amen" (Book of Common Prayer). □

## 7 In the Stocks, Singing

IN THE PAST FEW DAYS my husband and I have experienced the sudden arrest of activity that had been one form of our service to God. We are prevented from continuing. We are uncertain as to why this has happened and what we are to do.

Paul and Silas were arrested while they were proclaiming the gospel in Philippi and put into stocks. Not only was their work halted altogether, but they themselves were physically immobilized in a dungeon, held fast in stocks. What strange treatment for two earnest servants of God! What did they do? It would be quite understandable if they had raged or wept or sunk into depressed silence. Instead, they continued what for them had long since become habitual—they continued "at their prayer," and sang praises to God.

To the frantic question, *What do we do now?* there is a very simple reply: pray and sing. □

## 8 Power to Meet and to Give Thanks

OFTEN I PRAY FOR SOMEONE whose circumstances or needs are unknown to me. There are many prayers in Paul's letters which may be used for almost anyone. One of my favorites is in Colossians 1:9-12. A part of this prayer asks "May He strengthen you, in His glorious might, with ample power to meet whatever comes with fortitude, patience and joy, and to give thanks to the Father" (NEB).

That seems to cover every possibility. It does not ask for instant solutions or reversals. It does not call on God for miraculous deliverance out of any trouble that might come. It asks for a truly Christian response, by the sufficient power of God: to meet whatever comes as a true Christian should meet it, with the Holy Spirit's gifts of fortitude, patience, and joy. It asks for the power to give thanks. It *takes* power, doesn't it, to thank the Father when everything in us protests? But we find *in Him* (not always in what happens to us) plenty of reason to thank Him and plenty of power.  □

# 9 *Footprints of Faith*

IF WE LOOK FOR perfect models of faithfulness, we shall find one and only one—Jesus Christ. All others are flawed, for all others are sinners. Yet Abraham, who had his faults, is held up in the Letter to the Romans as a model of what faith is about. He took God at his word, when human hope was exhausted, "firm in the conviction of His power to do what He had promised" (Rom 4:21 NEB).

Walk, then, in those footprints. Don't try to *be* Abraham. Don't insist that God fulfill for you the promise given to Abraham. He is not going to make you the father of many nations. But hang on without giving place to the tiniest skepticism, to the promises given to all of us in Christ. "You are complete in Him" (Col 2:10 AV), for example. "Christ in you, the hope of glory" (Col 1:27 AV). "God shall supply all your need" (Phil 4:19 AV). "I will never leave thee nor forsake thee" (Heb 13:5 AV). Not to waver in your conviction that God means what He says is to walk in the footprints of faith.  □

## 10 Christ My Armor

WHEN FACED WITH THREAT of any sort of invasion or attack, whether from human or spiritual foes, it is quite natural to draw back, throw up my guard, attempt to defend myself. The Christian has a far better defense—"Let Christ Jesus Himself be the armor that you wear" (Rom 13:14 NEB). Let me take my stand *in* Him, come to my enemy without fear, responding only in the power and with the love of Christ. Who can hurt me then? And what hostility on earth or in hell can destroy me? That person whom I most dread to see, let me meet him as Christ meets him. Let *Christ* meet him. He is my armor, I am hidden in Him. My weakness, my fear, my hostility will be covered by his strength, his courage, his love.  □

## 11 God's Kingdom, My Reference Point

A BEGINNER'S PRAYERS are generally an attempt to get God to pay attention to his wants. As we grow in grace, prayer becomes an attempt to turn our attention to God. His kingdom becomes our reference point for every matter that concerns us. Will this thing further or hinder the working of the will of God in me, in those I pray for, in these situations? What is on my mind today? Let me bring it at once into the light of God's countenance, refer it to his scrutiny, lay it (and my heart with it) open before Him. If I am not prepared to submit something, I am interested in myself, not in the kingdom. "Set your mind on God's kingdom and His justice before everything else, and all the rest will come to you as well"(Mt 6:33 NEB).  □

# 12 Shut Up and Know

"DO THOU THYSELF but hold thy tongue for one day, and on the morrow how much clearer are thy purpose and duties," wrote Thomas Carlyle. The psalmist wrote (in Psalm 46) of great cataclysms, noise, war, destruction. What is the man of God supposed to do in the middle of all that? One thing above all else: "Be still and know that I am God" (Ps 46:10 AV). Simply shut up for a change. It is amazing what the quiet holding of the soul before the Lord will do to the external and seemingly uncontrollable tumult around us. It is in that stillness that the Voice will be heard, the only voice in all the universe that speaks peace to the deepest part of us.

No other voice than Thine has ever spoken,
  O Lord, to me—
No other words but Thine the stillness broken
  Of life's lone sea.
There openeth the spirit's silent chamber
  No other hand—
No other lips can speak the language tender,
  Speech of the Fatherland.
  (T.S.M., from *Hymns of Ter Steegen and Others*, Frances Bevan)  □

# 13 One Man's Godliness

LET US NEVER IMAGINE that to fear the Lord and find joy in his commandments make no real difference in the world. They matter. One man's godliness may well make the difference between another's shipwreck and his reaching the harbor, for a man who actually *enjoys* obeying God is "a beacon in darkness for honest men" (Ps 112:4 NEB).

Reading the biographies of men and women whose hearts were gladly given to God has lit the way for me. Seeing the obedience of just one simple Christian has more than once steered me clear of danger.

One of the old gospel songs my father taught us was P.P. Bliss':

Brightly beams our Father's mercy from His lighthouse evermore
But to us He gives the keeping of the lights along the shore.
Let the lower lights be burning, send a gleam across the wave—
Some poor struggling, fainting seaman, you may rescue, you may save.  □

## 14  Time for God's Will

ONE REASON we are so harried and hurried is that we make yesterday and tomorrow our business, when all that legitimately concerns us is today. If we really have too much to do, there are some items on the agenda which God did not put there. Let us submit the list to Him and ask Him to indicate which items we must delete. There is always time to do the will of God. If we are too busy to do that, we are too busy.

Lord, help me to take your yoke on my shoulder, not a yoke of my own making. May I learn from You to be gentle and humble-hearted. May I find that your load is light.  □

# 15 No Further than Natural Things

"WELL, IT'S PERFECTLY NATURAL for you to feel that way," I was telling myself when I was upset with the way someone had treated me. "It's a normal reaction."

It was a normal reaction for a carnal mind. It was not normal for a spiritual one. The carnal attitude deals with things on one level only—this world's. It "sees no further than natural things" (Rom 8:5 JBP).

Is there a telescope that will bring into focus things I would not see with merely "natural" vision? There is.

"The spiritual attitude reaches out after the things of the spirit." It is a different *means* of perceiving. It will enable me to see what I could not have seen with the naked—that is, the carnal—eye.

It works. When I looked at that person who had offended me through the "spiritual eye," I saw in him one of God's instruments to teach me, instead of one of the devil's to torment me. I saw something more. I saw a person God loves, and whom He wants to love through me.  □

# 16 We Carry Death and Life

WHEN JESUS LIVED ON EARTH, He lived in an ordinary man's body, carrying in that body both life and death. His thirty-three years of life were lived that He might die and through death forever destroy the power of death. He doesn't live here anymore. We do. We who believe *are* his Body, assigned to carry in our bodies the death He died. Paul said it (2 Cor 4:10 NEB). Insofar as we are willing to die, to 'cross out the self,' we carry the death Jesus died. But that isn't all! We carry also the life Jesus lived—the life that brings life to all, that will never end, that mysteriously is at work in the world because we who love Him are in the world.

O Life Eternal, purify this vessel of my body, that it may purely bear the death and life of Jesus for the life of the world. ☐

## 17 Weapons of Righteousness

THE MEANS OF CONQUERING the world, spiritually speaking, are not weapons of violence or organized power. In fact they are not thought of in the world as "weapons" at all, but as pitifully ineffective for obtaining any kind of victory. They are patience and kindliness, gifts of the Holy Spirit, sincere love, declaring the truth and the power of God. They are weapons which we wield in both hands, right and left (2 Cor 6:6, 7 NEB). The object of our conquest not being power, position, property, or personal satisfaction, the weapons required are not such as would be used by men seeking those things. Our Captain had one aim in dying for us—that we should cease to live for ourselves (2 Cor 5:15). This is our aim. Therefore our weapons will seem to those whose aim is worldly (i.e., "natural," and selfish), a strange set to choose. ☐

## 18 Wounds Can Change Your Heart

LIVING IN A WORLD broken by sin, we suffer wounds of many kinds. Perhaps the most painful are not the physical ones but those of the heart. No one has power to hurt us more deeply than somebody we love, somebody we counted on to understand and support us. But there are two ways to receive wounds. One leads to larger life. The other leads straight to death, that is to destruction—of those we influence as well as of ourselves.

By grace we can receive the wounds of our friends as our Master received them—in the strength and for the glory of our heavenly Father. Being sinners ourselves, however, we need to be brought low at the cross. Nothing will do this better than some piercing heart-wound, provided we seek Christ because of it and pray Him to purify us.

There is another way—the world's way. It is anger, resentment, retaliation, retreat into pride and self-justification. These are quite natural, and quite lethal. The choice is ours.

"The wound which is borne in God's way brings a change of heart too salutary to regret, but the hurt which is borne in the world's way brings death" (2 Cor 7:10 NEB). □


# 19 *The Root of Hostility to Others*

WHEN PERSONAL RELATIONSHIPS break down, it is a sure sign that there is some rift in one's relationship with God. The deeper the rift, the broader will be the effect on the human level. Rebellion against our Creator and Redeemer—against the One who designed us and gives us the breath of life and loves us every minute of every day—is not only unreasonable but outrageous. The sense of outrage will reveal itself in our treatment of others. We "get at" God by getting at those He has made, especially those whom his providence has placed close to us. We cannot bear the image of God in them, for we cannot bear the ineradicability of that image in our own being. It is a constant reminder of our own sin, which is the violation of the divine image. Without the consciousness of a legitimate claim on our lives, we could not know sin.

To recognize and submit to that claim is to return to peace and fellowship.

"If we claim to be sharing in his life while we walk in the dark, our words and our lives are a lie; but if we walk in the light as he himself is in the light, then we share together a common life, and we are being cleansed from every sin by the blood of Jesus His Son" (1 Jn 1:6, 7 NEB). □

# 20 Stars in a Dark World

ONE OF THE LETTERS the apostle Paul wrote from prison begs his friends to think and feel alike, to love, to have the "same turn of mind, and a common care for unity" (Phil 2:2 NEB). In such company there would be no room for rivalry or personal vanity. Each one would be thinking the others better, seeking to put their interests first.

Obedience, humility, cheerfulness ("Do all you have to do without complaint or wrangling") are rare in a warped and crooked world—nearly nonexistent, in fact, where each lives for his own ends. If a marriage counselor were to ask each partner, "What are your goals?" and the answer were "How can I best serve my husband or wife? What can I do to further *his or her* goals?" the counseling period would be over, the bill low. Any two people, any community of Christians who set themselves to look only to the other's interest would be a rare and radiant thing, shining, as Paul said, "like stars in a dark world" (Phil 2:15 NEB).

In that same sense, a Christian might well pray, "Lord, make me a star." □

# 21 A Smooth Path

THE WORK OF HEAVY HIGHWAY equipment is to smooth the way for travelers by exalting valleys, making low the mountains and hills, straightening the crooked. Obstacles—trees, rocks, houses, even mountains themselves—are put out of the way. This is what the Lord can do for his travelers (it is promised by the prophet Isaiah), but He does it without fuss, and in response to the one who simply *thinks* of Him: "Think of Him in all your ways, and He will smooth your path" (Prv 3:6 NEB).

The mind can build barriers, produce huge obstacles, collide with boulders of impossibility. Strangely and wonderfully, when we turn our thoughts to Him with whom nothing is an impossibility (and to *turn* thoughts takes an act of will), He smooths the path for us. We find it possible, maybe even easy, to move forward.

Don't waste time, energy, perhaps sleep-time, thinking of all those rocks in the way. Think of Him. Think of *Him*! You may find your path suddenly smoothed.  □

## 22  Power to Keep

THERE ARE TWO READINGS for 2 Tm 1:12—"I know who it is in whom I have trusted, and am confident of his power to keep safe *what he has put into my charge*" (NEB) or "*what I have put into his charge*." Christ has all the power needed to keep *anything* safe. What He gives me, or what I give Him, He can take care of. I can rest in perfect assurance, having that kind of coverage.

And—come to think of it—have I anything to put into his charge that He has not first put into mine? It all comes to the same thing. "What hast thou that thou didst not receive?" (1 Cor 4:7 AV).

Paul was writing from prison, where he was powerless to help those he loved or to look after things he cared for. No matter. He knew the One who is never powerless. He was sure of his power to keep.  □

## 23  Crowned Because He Suffered

OVER AND OVER in the Bible we are told that there is a correlation between suffering and glory. The reason lies deep in the mystery of evil, for of course there could be no suffering for creation, for beasts or men, or for the Son of Man, had not evil entered the world. But the story does not *end* with suffering.

"In Jesus we see one . . . crowned now with glory and honor because He suffered death" (Heb 2:9 NEB).

If we concentrate on that marvelous sequence, we will find in the midst of our own pain a great shaft of light. There is glory above us, shining down into our darkness, reminding us that "if we suffer *with Him*" (we need never suffer *without* Him, for He has entered into all our weakness, into death itself for us) "we shall also reign with him" (2 Tm 2:12 AV).

> His purposes will ripen fast,
> Unfolding every hour,
> The bud may have a bitter taste,
> But sweet will be the flower.
> (William Cowper)  □

## 24 *Do You Want an Answer?*

THIS IS THE QUESTION we need to ask ourselves when we are seeking "solutions" to our problems. Often we want only an audience. We want the chance to air grievances, to present our excuses, to make an explanation for our behavior, rather than a cure. More often than not the clearest and most direct answer can be found in the Word, but it must be sought honestly.

"The way of the Lord gives refuge to the honest man, but dismays those who do evil" (Prv 10:29 NEB).

We can approach God's word with a will to obey whatever it says to us about our present situation, or we can avoid it and say to anyone who would try to point us to it, "Don't throw the Book at me." The latter is an evasion, which supports our suspicion that our problems are, in fact, insoluble. The honest (i.e., humble) heart will indeed find the Lord's way to be a *refuge*.  □

# 25  What It Means to Be Human

IF JESUS HAD NOT BECOME MAN, we would not have known the full meaning of being men. He, whom Richard Crashaw described as the One "who in a Throne of stars Thunders above . . . He whom the Sun serves . . . He, the old Eternal Word" came to earth as a helpless newborn, utterly dependent on his mother. Humanity is dependence. Jesus grew up in a poor peasant home in an out-of-the-way village and learned obedience.

Adam and Eve rejected God's word and accepted Satan's. Their disobedience was their Declaration of Independence, which in fact meant the loss of the freedom God intended for them. It is by our acknowledging our own need, our helpless dependence on Him, that we may come to God. Learning that in Him we live and move and have our being, we are slowly conformed to his image. Thus and only thus, in what the old Puritans called "creaturely" dependence and obedience, we become fully human and fully free.

Lord Jesus, Master of my life, my very breath is in your hands. Remind me throughout the hours of this day to depend on You for the help I need and to ask You for it.

O what peace we often forfeit, O what needless pain we bear,
All because we do not carry everything to God in prayer.
(Joseph M. Scriven)  □


# 26  A Fine Thing

MOST OF US have never been anyone's slave in the literal sense, so we can hardly enter into Peter's meaning when he writes to servants who have suffered under perverse masters. But we know unkindness. We have been pained by someone's lack of consideration or unjust criticism.

Why is this happening to me? is a question most of us occasionally ask. If we ask it petulantly, there is nothing particularly creditable about our attitude. The apostle Peter wrote to those slaves who were at the mercy of abusive masters. "When you have behaved well and suffer for it, your fortitude is a fine thing in the sight of God. To that you were called, because Christ suffered on your behalf" (1 Pt 2:20 NEB), was his encouragement to them. His answer to the "why" is just this: to that you were called. If we endure merely because we savor the notion of being martyrs, there is nothing fine in that. There is nothing fine in brooding on the pain itself and how sorely we have been put upon. The fine thing is for God so to occupy our thoughts that it is really nothing to us whether others treat us well or ill. Think on Christ: how was He treated? How do your sufferings compare with his? That will give a different perspective, I think.

Let's not be surprised at our difficulties, even if—no, especially if—we encounter them when we are truly seeking to obey the Lord. There are two kingdoms in deadly opposition to each other. If we do anything to further the kingdom of God, we may expect to find what Christ found on that road—abuse, indifference, injustice, misunderstanding, trouble of some kind. Take it. Why not? *To that you were called.* In Latin America someone who feels sorry for himself is said to look like a donkey in a downpour. If we think of the glorious fact that we are on the same path with Jesus, we might see a rainbow.  □

## 27 *When the River Bursts*

PSYCHOLOGISTS CHART "stress factors" related to various kinds of emotional trauma and the response of different people to those factors—death, divorce, job loss, illness, and such which threaten the very foundations of people's lives. What can hold us at such times?

In a simple story Jesus showed the secret of stability. One man comes to Jesus, hears Him, and acts on what he hears. He is like the man who builds a house on solid rock. Another man hears (is exposed to the same truth, given equal opportunity) but does not act (does not choose to act) on the word he hears. Jesus said he is building a house on sand. When floods come, the river bursts upon it (Lk 6:49 NEB), the house collapses and falls with a great crash.

What sort of floods was He talking about? What rivers might be likely to burst over a man's house? Surely He meant the stresses of life, not terribly different from the stresses we experience, anything that shakes the foundations. It is at such times that we become aware of what those foundations are. Have we laid them on the Rock that never moves, or have we, merely by not obeying the word we have heard, been laying them on sand? That sand is the self—shifty, unstable, carried back and forth by conflicting currents (popular opinions, for example?), utterly undependable and incapable of holding up under pressure.

Lead me, Lord, to the Rock that is higher than I. Let me hear your word, give me grace to obey, to build steadily, stone upon stone, day by day, to do what You say. Establish my heart where floods have no power to overwhelm, for Christ's sake. Amen. □

## 28 Death Shall Not Hold Us

THE POWER OF THE RESURRECTION is a power that vanquishes every other power in heaven or earth. The battle was the bitterest ever fought, but death was the loser, Jesus the Victor. Because "the tomb could not hold Him; snapped like a straw death's omnipotent bars" (Amy Carmichael: *Edges of His Ways*, p. 192), sin and death and sorrow need not hold us either. The same power is available to us if we will take it by faith.

There are many tombs where we may be held if we succumb to the powers of sin and death. Hatred, self-pity, bitterness, resentment—these are tombs. By the power that raised Jesus Christ from that sealed and guarded tomb we may be delivered from whatever seals us off from life. Jesus came to give us life, nothing less than life, "abundant" life.

Do you know someone you are praying for who is living in the darkness of such a tomb? Has it seemed that there is no more possibility of getting through to him than to someone buried? Resentment has sealed him off from any approach. Pray for the power of the resurrection to release him. Refuse, by the grace of God, to be held back by his bitterness. Then ask the Lord to help you to meet him next time in the consciousness of *Christ risen*. Instead of dreading the meeting because of the thought of former disastrous meetings, face it with joy. Christ is risen! Christ is risen!

"May the God of peace, who brought up from the dead our Lord Jesus, the great Shepherd of the sheep, by the blood of the eternal covenant, make us perfect in all goodness so that we may do his will; and may he make of us what he would have us be through Jesus Christ, to whom be glory forever and ever. Amen" (Heb 13:20, 21 NEB). □

## 29 *The Arbiter Is Peace*

WHEN THERE ARE DISPUTES or differences of any sort between people, there are four possible results: estrangement, an armed truce, compromise, or reconciliation. The first of these is the reason for a good many divorces. The second accounts for many unhappy marriages. The third may seem the best that can be hoped for. The fourth is what Christians are called to, always. In marital disputes, or those between labor and management, an arbiter is sometimes called in, often after much wrangling and bitterness. An arbiter has absolute power to judge and decide.

There is a another arbiter, too often forgotten. "Let Christ's peace be arbiter in your hearts; to this peace you were called" (Col 3:15 NEB).

Wouldn't it make an astonishing difference in our fellowship with one another if we would let that peace arbitrate, if we would remember the promised parting gift of Christ, "My peace I give you," and the command to live at peace with all?

But, we ask, how? How does it work? The context in Colossians shows us:

> You are God's chosen race, his saints; he loves you, and you should be clothed in sincere compassion, in kindness and humility, gentleness and patience. Bear with one another; forgive each other as soon as a quarrel begins. The Lord has forgiven you; now you must do the same. Over all these clothes, to keep them together and complete them, put on love. (Col 3:12-14 JB)

Are we willing to follow Him here? He will help us if we are. He will calm the troubled waters.  □

## 30 The Face of Jesus

THE FACE of Jesus:
marred more than any man—
spit upon,
slapped,
thorn-pierced,
bloodied,
sweating,
the beard plucked,
twisted in pain—
For my salvation.

A glorious face, now.

Let its light shine on me, O Light of Life.
Let Your radiance fall on me, Sun and Savior,
Lighten my darkness.
Then grant me this by Your grace:
That I, in turn, may give
"The light of the knowledge of the glory of God" (2 Cor 4:6 AV)
As I see it in the face of Jesus Christ.  □

## 31 *Pray with Jesus*

BECAUSE I AM "OF THE EARTH, earthy," I find that my prayers for
the people I love are mostly bound by very earthy concerns—
Lord, help P. to find a good wife, show G. which college to attend,
provide money for W.'s house and E.'s car, help T. with his book,
give X. a better job. It is meet and proper to pray for such things,
but not to pray *only* for such things. There are prayers of far
more lasting import which we must also learn to pray. We can
find words for those in the prayer of Jesus for the people He
loved:

1. that they may be one;
2. that they may find his joy completed in themselves;
3. that they may be kept from evil;
4. that they may be made holy by the truth;
5. that they may live in Christ;
6. that they may grow complete into one;
7. that they may be with him;
8. that the love which God has for Christ may be in their
hearts.

If we learn to pray that kind of prayer, it will perhaps amend
the "lesser" prayers.

Lord, teach me to pray. Open my eyes to see beyond the
earthly to the heavenly. Let my primary concerns be heavenly
ones, that your kingdom may come on earth, your will be done
in me and in those I love. Teach me to pray with Jesus, for his
sake. Amen.  □

# 1 Pick Up Your Cross

JESUS INVITES US to be his disciples. If we choose to accept his loving invitation, we must understand that there are certain conditions to be fulfilled. One of them is a willingness to accept the cross. Is this a once-for-all taking up of one particular burden? I don't think so. It seems to me that my "cross" is each particular occasion when I am given the chance to "die"—that is, to offer up my own will whenever it crosses Christ's. This happens very often. A disagreement with my husband can cause an argument and harsh words, even if the matter is ridiculously small—"When are you going to get that dashboard light fixed in the car?" I have already mentioned the light three times. It may be time to keep my mouth shut, but I don't want to keep my mouth shut. Here, then, is a chance to die. A decision which affects both of us may be a fairly big one, but we find ourselves on two sides of the fence. One of us, then, must "die." It is never easy for me. Shall I make excuses for myself (that's the way I am; it's my personality; it's the way I was raised; I'm tired; I can't hack it; it doesn't turn me on; you don't understand)—or shall I pick up this cross?

Perhaps my illustration seems to trivialize the cross of Christ. His was so unimaginably greater. What cross could I possibly take up which would be analogous? Just here is the lesson for me: when Jesus took up his cross, He was saying yes with all his being to the will of the Father. If I am unwilling to say yes in even a very little thing, how shall I accept a more painful thing? What sort of practice does it take for a disciple to learn to follow the Crucified? A friend hurts us, a plan goes awry, an effort fails—small things indeed. But then cancer strikes, a daughter marries unwisely, a business folds, a wife abandons her home and family. The call still comes to us: Take up your cross and come with Me. With You, Lord? Yes, with Me. Will You give me strength and show me the way? That was my promise—is it my custom to break promises? □

# 2 No Other Choice

NO CHRISTIAN EVER GETS beyond the power of temptation as long as he lives in "this mortal coil." Jesus was not beyond it—who are we that we should become more spiritual than Jesus? If we say that we have been delivered forever from sin, we are deceiving ourselves. We are never in a more vulnerable spot than when someone sins against us. All the "old Adam" in us rises up to retaliate. Perhaps we control the urge to punch the person or even to retort with the withering words that spring to mind. But then we wake up in the night and think about all the ways we could put this individual in his place—polite ways, we tell ourselves, Christian ways, but put him in his place we certainly will. The still small voice asks: Is that Christlike?

"The love of Christ leaves us no choice. . . . His purpose in dying for all was that men, while still in life, should cease to live for themselves" (2 Cor 5:14, 15 NEB).

No other choice but love. Cease to live for yourself. Live for Christ. Don't bother singing, "Oh, how I love Jesus" as long as you are plotting retaliation. You don't really have that choice, not if you're a Christian.  □

# 3 Surrender Every Thought

"ALTHOUGH OF COURSE we lead normal human lives, the battle we are fighting is on the spiritual level. The very weapons we use are not those of human warfare but powerful in God's warfare for the destruction of the enemy's strongholds. Our battle is to bring down every deceptive fantasy. . . . We fight to capture every thought until it acknowledges the authority of Christ" (2 Cor 10:4-6 JBP).

As I was praying this morning these words were in my mind.

There were other things in my mind as well, things which had certainly not acknowledged the authority of Christ. I had been praying for months: Lord, have mercy on So-and-So. There was evidence that He was answering that prayer, and, far from being thankful for that, I found in my heart Jonah's anger. Why should God be merciful to the people of Nineveh or to this person? They didn't deserve it!

Right then and there the spiritual battle was drawn. Whose side was I on anyway? Everything that was opposed to God and his purposes had to be surrendered. I had been trying to explain to God why my own feelings ought to be considered, why his were all wrong. That, too, had to be captured, made to acknowledge Christ's authority. A surrendered mind is not one which is no longer in operation. It is, rather, a mind freed from rebellion and opposition. To be Christ's captive is to be perfectly free. □

## 4 *Your Troubles—Whose Fault?*

I NEVER NOTICED until this morning the context of this command in the Epistle of James: "My brothers, do not blame your troubles on one another or you will fall under judgment" (Jas 5:9 NEB). The context is *patience*. A farmer's precious crop comes up only as he waits patiently for autumn rains, winter snows, spring sunshine. Anything worth having is worth waiting for. Troubles are permitted in order to teach us many lessons, not the least of which is patience. If we instantly assign responsibility for those troubles to somebody else, our energies will go into resentment instead of into learning God's lesson of patient waiting. The Lord's coming is far more certain than even autumn rains and winter snows. We can stand firm and patient no matter how others treat us, knowing that in the end our troubles will be transformed. "The Lord is full of pity and compassion" (Jas 5:11)—can we believe that, even when we feel sorry for ourselves because we are so badly treated? He knows it all. He purposes a crop. Be patient. It will come.  □

# 5 Exert Yourselves

THE VIGOR OF OUR RESPONSE reveals how much we care about something. If a man is stung by a bee, he cares. It takes very little time for him to respond. When taxes are raised, howls of complaint follow rather quickly. The winner of a state lottery presents himself without delay.

Salvation is a free gift. It includes everything that makes for life and godliness, here and hereafter. What is it worth? It's beyond calculation, priceless. We share in the very being of God. Um hmm, we say. How do we get it? Oh—by faith. Yes. Very simple. Accept Jesus. The price is all paid. My sins are forgiven. I'm on the "Hallelujah Train."

All true. That is the gospel. But that is not all. Gifts must be received, possessed, and fostered. God's choice and calling, we must clinch. This is an aspect of the gospel which many Christians (Protestants in particular) have overlooked. The apostle Peter writes, "Exert yourselves to clinch God's choice and calling.... Thus you will be afforded full and free admission into the eternal kingdom" (2 Pt 1:10, 11 NEB). How do I "exert myself"? Peter tells us: "Try your hardest to supplement your faith with virtue [right action and thinking], virtue with knowledge, knowledge with self-control, self-control with fortitude," etc. (2 Pt 1:5-7). Check that passage. It is still true that nothing can wash away my sin but the blood of Jesus. It is also true that God gives us responsibility—that is, the obligation to respond. How much do we care? The vigor of our response will reveal how much.  □

## 6 The Calm Spirit of Christ

TODAY IS MOVING DAY. There will be plenty of reason for fretting and stewing, impatience, and turbulence. I am one who seems to feel that unless I do things or unless they are done my way, they will not be done right, and the day will disintegrate. But I have been watching the sea—very turbulent this morning because of a tropical storm hundreds of miles away—and I remember Him whose word was enough to calm it.

Speak that word to me today, dear Lord: *peace*. Let your calm spirit, through the many potentially rough minutes of this day, in every task, say to my soul, *Be still*. Even this day's chaos, with all its clutter and exertion, will be ordered by your quiet power if my heart is subject to your word of peace. Thank You, Lord. □

## 7 The Focus of Faith

IN ONE OF THE PHOTO ALBUMS from my years in Ecuador is a close-up of a big scorpion on a window screen. I know what was beyond that ugly thing—a green lawn set about with palm trees, a garden of pineapples, a sweep of pasture land, and then the curve of a wide river. The photograph knows nothing of all that. The photographer had focused on the scorpion. He got a very good picture of a scorpion. The eye of the camera saw nothing else.

The eye of faith looks through and past that which the human eye focuses on. Faith looks at the facts—even the ugly ones (remember Abraham who looked at his wife's barrenness and his own impotence)—but does not stop there. It looks beyond to the beauty of things the human eye can never see—things as invisible as the palms and the pineapples are in my photograph.

When the eye of the heart is fixed on the world and the self, everything eternal and invisible is blurred and obscure. No wonder we cannot recognize God—we are studying the scorpion. Instead of gazing at Him in all his majesty and love, we peer at the screen, horrified at what we see there.

Blessed are the pure in heart, for they shall see God. Make my heart pure, Lord, that I may will to do your will. Give me the courage to see my world with all its evil and pain, but change the focus of my life.

> Lord Jesus, make Thyself to me
> A living, bright reality,
> More present to faith's vision keen
> Than any outward object seen,
> More dear, more intimately nigh
> Than e'en the sweetest earthly tie.
>
> (J.B. French)  □

## 8 Cosmic Orphans

MODERN MAN HAS BEEN DESCRIBED as a "cosmic orphan." He no longer knows the Father of us all and feels isolated and bewildered in an ever-expanding universe. The diameter of our own galaxy is 100,000 light years, and astronomers tell us that the farthest object they can see in the universe is perhaps ten billion (billion!) light years away. Such distances, the enormity of that space, are awesome, even terrifying to those who feel orphaned. The huge advances of scientific knowledge serve only to notify us of how huge our ignorance is.

> When we've explored ten thousand worlds
> By scientific scan,
> Omniscience still belongs to God
> As always—not to man.

The prophet Isaiah wrote that with the span of the palm of his hand God "set limits to the heavens." To Him coasts and islands weigh as little as specks of dust. "Lift up your eyes to the heavens; consider who created it all, led out their host one by one and called them all by their names.... Do you not know, have you not heard? The Lord, the everlasting God, creator of the wide world ... gives vigor to the weary, new strength to the exhausted" (Is 40:12, 15, 26, 28, 29 NEB).

If God can fling out a galaxy so that it stays where He wants it and yet observes one exhausted person and strengthens him, can we believe that we are adrift in a fathomless void? Hear the promise of Jesus: "No, I will not abandon you or leave you as orphans in the storm—I will come to you" (Jn 14:18 LB). □

## 9 One of the Mysteries of Our Humanity

HAVE YOU EVER THOUGHT much about the fact that we, created by God for his own pleasure and glory, are permitted by the Creator Himself to deny Him? Even though we are totally dependent on Him for our next breath, with that breath we may declare that He does not exist or that we refuse to do what He wants us to do. We live by the life He gives us, moment by moment. We enjoy rain, sunshine, the growth of crops and flowers, sensations, delights, satisfactions of many kinds. Yet we often act as though we were sufficient in ourselves, needing no interference from Him. I can, by the power mysteriously granted me by my Creator and Redeemer, declare myself master of my fate, captain of my soul, and say, *My will be done.* That the Lord should expose Himself to this effrontery in a million forms, for millions of days and nights, is the mystery of love and grace. Still He draws us with cords of love, calls us to come, waits (amazing grace) for us to bow and say, *My Lord and my God!* □

# 10 Christ Is Message and Messenger

EVERY WORD SPOKEN by Jesus must be understood by the *life* of Jesus. The one cannot be separated from the other. If we attempt to understand what He said without reference to what He did, we do violence to God's revelation of Himself. Here are some examples:

"Give up your right to yourself." Can this mean self-destruction, masochism, obliteration of the personality? See the perfect Son of God, exercising his human will in the fullness of its God-given power, as He *offers* Himself, pours out his soul unto death. What *life* streams from that *giving up.* What strength springs from his weakness.

"The truth shall make you free" (Jn 8:32 AV)—words often wrested away from their context ("If you continue in my word, you are truly my disciples, and you will know the truth and the truth will make you free")and also away from the Man who spoke them. His life, his every act, was perfectly free. It was free because He heard the Word of the Father, did what He saw Him do, and knew Him. His freedom was the result of his obedience. There is no shortcut to our freedom. We must live the life Christ lived—a life of faith, a will offered to the Father, daily obedience. □

# 11 Limitations Are Gifts

YESTERDAY AS I WAS READING my brother Tom's book, *The Achievement of C.S. Lewis,* I was admiring again the scope of his knowledge, his ability to comprehend another's genius, and his wonderful command of English. By contrast my own limitations seemed severe indeed. They are of many kinds—analytical, critical, articulatory, not to mention educational. But my limitations, placing me in a different category from Tom

Howard's or anyone else's, become, in the sovereignty of God, gifts. For it is with the equipment that I have been given that I am to glorify God. It is *this* job, not that one, that He gave me.

For some, the limitations are not intellectual but physical. The same truth applies. Within the context of their suffering, with whatever strength they have, be it ever so small, they are to glorify God. The apostle Paul actually claimed that he "gloried" in infirmities, because it was there that the power of Christ was made known to him.

If we regard each limitation which we are conscious of today as a gift—that is, as one of the terms of our particular service to the Master—we won't complain or pity or excuse ourselves. We will rather offer up those gifts as a sacrifice, *with thanksgiving.*  □


## 12 Nobody Knows the Trouble I've Seen

WHEN WE BEGIN TO IMAGINE that our own problems are so deep, so insoluble, or so unusual that no one really understands us, we delude ourselves. It is one of the many delusions of pride, for Scripture tells us not only that our High Priest, Christ, has been tempted in every way as we are, but that no temptation has ever come our way that is not common to man. There are no more new temptations than there are new sins. Our story, whatever it is, is an old one, and He who has walked the human road has entered fully into our experiences of sorrow and pain and has overcome them. He has comforted others in our situation, gone with them into the same furnaces and lions' dens, has brought them out without smell of fire or mark of tooth.

It is a bad thing to take refuge in difficulties, thus excusing ourselves from responsibility to others because we think our situation is unique. If we are willing to receive help, our Helper is standing by—sometimes in the form of another human being sent by Him, qualified by Him to help us. It may be a case of our not receiving help because we were too proud to receive the kind God sent. Sometimes we really prefer to wallow.

"Ours is not a high priest unable to sympathize with our weaknesses, but one who, because of his likeness to us, has been tested every way, only without sin. Let us therefore boldly approach the throne of our gracious God, where we may receive mercy and in his grace find timely help" (Heb 4:15, 16 NEB).  □

# 13 Die Quickly

TO HOLD ONTO SOMETHING with a desperate grip is not the way to die. Death is a painful process, and restoratives offered to the dying wretch bound to his wheel only prolong his agony. There are times when the thing to do is simply to die. I am thinking, of course, of dying to the self. We clutch so tenaciously to our rights, hopes, ambitions, something to which God has perhaps said a plain no. If would-be comforters offer us consolation and sympathy, if they assist us to strengthen our grasp when it should be loosened, they do not love us as God loves us. The way into life is death, and if we refuse it we are refusing Him who showed us that way and no other. The love which is strong as death is not only willing to save the beloved, it is willing to seem, if necessary, pitiless, insensitive, unloving, if that is what will help the beloved to die—that is, to be released from the bondage of self, which is death, and thus enter the gateway of life.

Archbishop Fenelon wrote to the countess of Montberon, "You want to die, but to die without any pain. . . . You must give all or nothing when God asks it. If you have not the courage to give, at least let Him take."  □

# 14 One Cause of Collapse

ONE EXCUSE THAT IS A CATCH-ALL for any failure to do our jobs is "burn-out." It's an occupational hazard in just about every occupation modern man has ever heard of. Strangely enough, we never heard about burn-out until the past couple of decades, but now everybody suffers from it. Exhaustion—physical, mental, emotional—is endemic. Why?

One reason is lack of humility. In our anxiety to compete, to prove ourselves, to be a success as the world defines it, we are wearied and overburdened. If we sought instead only the greatness of the kingdom, we would become childlike. The truly important things are hidden from the clever and intelligent and are shown to those who are willing to come and be shown, to put on the yoke Christ bears, which is the will of the Father. We need to learn to walk side by side with Him, bearing humbly and gently the yoke He places on us, not the unbearable burdens of competition and recognition and something called fulfillment. If we do this, any burden He allows—of loss or pain or insult or responsibility or heartbreak—will be both bearable and light, for the weight is shared with Him. No yoke laid on us in this way will cause us to burn out or collapse. This yoke itself will in fact be the very means of our finding rest. There is no form of recreation or relaxation or therapy to compare with the rest, the gentle ease, of Christ's yoke. "Come," He says to us, "and learn of Me." □

# 15 The Real Test of Love

IT IS NOT DIFFICULT to imagine, in certain moods and settings, that we love people. We may feel expansive and good-natured for a variety of reasons—our own good health or digestion, for example, or beautiful weather, comfortable circumstances, nice folks doing nice things for us. The Bible is a sword that cuts through mere sentiment. It tells us that the accurate test of our love for God's *children* is obedience to *God*. "By this we know that we love the children of God, when we love God and obey His commandments" (1 Jn 5:2 RSV). It is an objective test, not a subjective one. Love as the Bible defines it is perceptible through action rather than through mere feeling. It is not, as Eric Alexander of Scotland put it, a "glandular condition."

Much of the talk nowadays about loving one another is soupy and silly. It will not stand the biblical test. Love for people goes hand-in-hand with love for God—if you don't love the brother you see, how can you love the God you don't see? Loving God requires submission to his discipline—He rebukes, chastens, refines with fire, purifies by trial. Do we love Him enough to say yes to all that? Do we love others enough to encourage endurance in them?

Jesus, Thou art all compassion,
Pure, unbounded Love Thou art;
Visit us with Thy salvation,
Enter every trembling heart.
(Charles Wesley)

# 16  *The Fear of Loss*

IN C.S. LEWIS' *Screwtape Letters* we see with startling clarity the cleverness of the enemy in deceiving human beings. Selfishness has a thousand forms, most of which we are slow to recognize for what they are. I was thinking about the fear of loss and what a stranglehold it can have on me. As I listed some of the things I dreaded to lose, it occurred to me that this fear is a deadly form of selfishness. Selfishness does terrible things to us, but it does not stop there. It does terrible things to others. "Saving our own skin" usually results in skinning somebody else. Think, for example, of the fear of losing: reputation, opportunity for advancement, credit, recognition, position, beauty, youth, health, money, the love of friends or children, compliments, popularity, security, privacy, rights, people you love, job, home, dreams, power.

As I considered each of these separately, I began to think what sort of sin each kind of loss tempts me to commit. Then I thought about what kind of faith is required to enable me to commit those fears to God. Has He, in fact, made provision for these things? The list is not a list of sins—make no mistake about that. It is a list of blessings, of gifts from God. But to grasp them selfishly and greedily, to hang onto them fiercely and allow myself to be enslaved by the fear of losing them, is to deny Christ. Do not fear, He says to us. *I am with you.*  □

# 17  *Freedom from Fear*

THERE IS A SENSE in which every form of fear is essentially the fear of death. Jesus came to deliver us from that in all its forms. "He became a human being so that by going through death as a man he might destroy him who had the power of death, that is, the devil; and might also set free those who lived their whole lives a prey to the fear of death" (Heb 2:14, 15 JBP).

I know people whose lives are totally controlled by fear. There is no bondage more powerful and crippling. Fear takes over the mind, coercing and circumscribing all its activity. We know where that spirit of fear originates, and we know the name of the enemy who would hold us enslaved. In the name of our God we must tread down our enemies, including all the nagging "what ifs" of our lives. To those frightening possibilities Christ answers, "I will never leave you or forsake you." Let the very worst thing come to pass—even there, *especially* there, his hand will hold us. If we go into darkness, He is there, has been there before us, has conquered all its powers. That's why He became a man. That's why He died. That's why He rose again.

My Lord and my God—forgive my fears. Deliver me from bondage by the power of your resurrection. ☐

## 18 The Rupture of Self

SOMETIMES OUR PRAYERS are for deliverance from conditions which are morally indispensable—that is, conditions which are absolutely necessary to our redemption. God does not grant us those requests. He will not because He loves us with a pure and implacable purpose: that Christ be formed in us. If Christ is to live in my heart, if his life is to be lived in me, I will not be able to contain Him. The self, small and hard and resisting as a nut, will have to be ruptured. My own purposes and desires and hopes will have to at times be exploded. The rupture of the self is death, but out of death comes life. The acorn must rupture if an oak tree is to grow.

It will help us to remember, when we do not receive the answer we hoped for, that it is morally necessary, morally indispensable, that some of our prayers be denied, "that the life of Jesus may be plainly seen in these bodies of ours" (2 Cor 4:11 JBP). Then think of this: the agonized prayer of Jesus in the garden went unanswered, too. Why? In order that life—our life—might spring forth from death—his death. ☐

## 19 Adversaries

THE PSALMS ARE FULL of prayers to God to defeat adversaries—nations, foes, enemies. The Lord of hosts (also translated the Lord of the armies of heaven) is called upon to arise and conquer. People who live in a country not at war may tend to skip over such prayers as not applicable to them, unless they recognize as an adversary anything or anyone that would defeat the purpose of God. Adverse circumstances affect us all, and we feel as helpless as the Israelites, hotly pursued by the cavalry, infantry, horses, and chariots of Egypt. As I write this, it happens that we find ourselves impotent to untangle a certain legal matter—helpless before the delays, the refusal to accept responsibility, the apparent dilatoriness of the attorneys involved. Money is being wasted, people's rights ignored; frustrations abound.

> The peoples shake their heads at us; . . .
> I am covered with shame. . . .
> But we do not forget Thee, . . .
> We have not gone back on our purpose. . . .
> Bestir Thyself, Lord; why dost Thou sleep? . . .
> Arise and come to our help;
> For Thy love's sake set us free.
> (Ps 44:14, 15, 17, 18, 23, 26 NEB)

If it were not for the adversaries who make us conscious of our impotence, how would we learn to trust God's omnipotence?

Lord of the armies of heaven, I praise You for your power to conquer. Teach me to trust your power, not mine.  □

## 20 Spiritual Transport

MOST OF US EXPERIENCE from time to time happy feelings that we think are somehow religious. We feel that we are in a special way in touch with the divine. Our hearts are "strangely warmed." But most of life is not like this. We do not live on the Mount of Transfiguration. We are not riding continually in chariots of fire.

When Jesus was preparing his disciples for his departure from them, He said, "Believe in God. Believe also in me."

The obedience of faith requires that we do our work. We must go on day after day, simply and humbly, not waiting for chills and thrills. Grace, not revelation, is our daily bread. Grace is enough. Receiving that, in the portion given according to the lovingkindness of our God, we must act responsibly in the situation in which He puts us, as the disciples had to do when left behind at Christ's ascension. No doubt they felt bewildered and abandoned and would like to have risen with Him through the clouds. When the angels suddenly stood beside them and asked why they were gazing into the sky, they "came down to earth," as it were, went back to Jerusalem to the lodging where they belonged and carried on with their prayers.

Lord, help me today to receive what You want me to have and to do my work as a good and faithful servant. □

## 21 Not Power but Privilege

JESUS GAVE RESPONSIBILITY and power to those who were willing to take the path He took. They were to represent the kingdom wherever they went—their peace to rest on those who received them. Those who rejected them were actually rejecting Christ. His followers would have power over snakes and scorpions.

There are principles here for us today, I believe. Surely every believer represents Christ and his kingdom. We are promised power from the Holy Spirit. But as soon as his power is manifest, another spirit is there instantly to tempt us to take credit to ourselves. If we are thanked for something we were merely the instrument for, it can become a heady business. Wow! we say, imagining that we deserve the credit.

Jesus warned the disciples not to be impressed when spirits submitted to them. It was not by their might or power that the enemy was subdued. They were nothing more than bearers of the kingdom. He told them to rejoice, not that they had performed a miraculous feat, but that their names were written in heaven.

Open my eyes, Lord, to recognize that the power is always yours. What is mine is the privilege, given from above, for your glory. □

## 22 Courage to Love

GOD'S LOVE HOLDS us to the highest. This was the kind of love Amy Carmichael of India prayed for and taught to the children on Dohnavur—this love, the kind wherewith God loved us. "Hold one another to the highest," she told them. God's purpose was to lift us out of ourselves, out of the miry clay, and set our feet on a rock. We are not saviors, but we can help others toward faith. This means not only loving them while they're still in the mire, but loving them out of it. We must love them as they are and love them enough to draw them higher.

Someone has said that the best thing a father can do for his children is to love their mother. This demonstration far outshines all the homilies he can preach at them. By daily example he holds them to the highest. Jesus said, "For their sakes I sanctify myself" (Jn 17:19 AV). His holy obedience to the Father saved us. Our holy obedience to the Father makes a difference to those we love.

Lord, give me the courage to love as You loved me.  □

## 23 The Lust for Security

ONCE WE HAVE SET ourselves to be pilgrims and strangers on the earth, which is what Christians are meant to be, it is incongruous for us to continue to insist upon the sort of security the world tries to guarantee. Our security lies not in protecting ourselves from suffering, but in putting ourselves fully into the hands of God. The desire for physical and material security makes us sly and hard. No. We must be like little children. The child in its father's arms is not worried. It lies quietly at rest because it trusts its father.

We disobey sometimes because we say it is impossible to do

what God asks. Impossible? Perhaps what we mean is impossible to do that and keep our security, impossible to obey without tremendous cost, or at least tremendous risk. Where, then, will we find safety? Is it likely that we will find it *elsewhere* than in the arms of the Father?

Teach me to rest in your everlasting arms. Make me know that all other security is illusion.  □

## 24 *How Far to Go*

WE SAY THAT WE ARE WILLING to follow Jesus. Peter said he would go with Him to prison and to death, not expecting that either would likely be required. Let us settle it once and for all—to follow Him will mean death. Not crucifixion in the literal sense, probably, but the coming to the end of ourselves, our expectations, our dreams. He must bring us to that end in order to bring us to the beginning of the Christ-life. "I am crucified with Christ, nevertheless I live," was Paul's testimony (Gal 2:20 AV).

But does this mean none of my hopes will be fulfilled? Is it all wilderness and sorrow? The people of Israel must have asked this while en route to Canaan. Must we follow so far? And when they were desperate for water, God led them to Marah where the water was bitter. Terrible disappointment. But then—the miracle of the tree that made it sweet!

How far shall we go with Him who calls us to fellowship with Himself? Shall we stop dead in our tracks if the water is bitter? Shall we turn tail and run if we glimpse a cross? "Whoever cares for his own safety is lost" (Mt 16:25 NEB). Think of missing the miracle of the water. Think of missing the resurrection.

Savior Christ, I want to go the whole way. Keep me from faltering today. Show the tree that transforms bitter water, and help me to live in its shade.  □

## 25 How to Do the Job You Don't Really Want to Do

CERTAIN ASPECTS OF THE JOB the Lord has given me to do are very easy to postpone. I make excuses, find other things that take precedence, and, when I finally get down to business to do it, it is not always with much grace. A new perspective has helped me recently:

The job has been given to me to do.

Therefore it is a gift.

Therefore it is a privilege.

Therefore it is an offering I may make to God.

Therefore it is to be done gladly, if it is done for Him.

Therefore it is the route to sanctity. Here, not somewhere else, I may learn God's way. In this job, not in some other, God looks for faithfulness. The discipline of this job is, in fact, the chisel God has chosen to shape me with—into the image of Christ.

Thank you, Lord, for the work You have assigned me. I take it as your gift; I offer it back to you. With your help I will do it gladly, faithfully, and I will trust You to make me holy.  □

## 26 Spiritual Playpens

LOVE IS THE WAY to maturity. Selfishness stunts growth and keeps us in a spiritual playpen. The world is full of emotional babies, crawling over each other, screaming, "Mine! This I want, and this I shall have, and never mind what it does to anybody else!" What a relief, what peace, when one who has reached spiritual adulthood, who by love has grown out of himself, comes along. He freely gives up his own aims and ambitions, his safety and his cherished plans, his possessions, his feelings, anything at all that will help and says *my life for yours*. Such a one comes as a rescuer.

To give myself up is the last thing I think of doing. It looks like weakness. In God's eyes, though, it is power.

"We who share His weakness shall by the power of God live with Him in your service" (2 Cor 13:4 NEB).  □

## 27 The Source and the Course

"IF THE SPIRIT IS THE SOURCE of our life, let the Spirit also direct our course" (Gal 5:25 NEB).

It is only reasonable that He who gives and sustains our life (the Source) should be the One we would want to follow (whose Course we would choose). But we are not very reasonable creatures, I'm afraid. Which side am I on—the self or the Spirit? I don't always know. But I can check myself out by studying the list of the kind of behavior that belongs to the lower nature (fornication, impurity, indecency, idolatry, sorcery, quarrels, contentious temper, envy, fits of rage, selfish ambitions, dissensions, party intrigues, jealousies, drinking bouts, orgies) and comparing it to the list of the "harvest of the Spirit" (love, joy, peace, patience, kindness, goodness, fidelity, gentleness, self-control). If I pinpoint from those two lists what characterizes my behavior today, it's easy enough to identify the source.  □

## 28 Identity

THE SEARCH FOR RECOGNITION hinders faith. We cannot believe so long as we are concerned with the "image" we present to others. When we think in terms of "roles" for ourselves and others, instead of simply doing the task given us to do, we are thinking as the world thinks, not as God thinks. The thought of Jesus was always and only for the Father. He did what He saw the Father do. He spoke what He heard the Father say. His will was submitted to the Father's will.

"You have no love for God in you," He said to the Pharisees. "I have come accredited by my Father, and you have no welcome for me. . . . How can you have faith so long as you receive honor from one another, and care nothing for the honor that comes from him who alone is God?" (Jn 5:42-44 NEB).  □

## 29 First Be Quiet

OUR HECTIC LIVES involve many changes, and changes require decisions, and decisions must often be made in the midst of a multitude of confusions. We run here and there asking advice. Often we make decisions without sufficient deliberation because we simply haven't time—or so we tell ourselves.

There is a marvelously helpful practice that we usually overlook. It is quietness. Notice how often in the gospels we find Jesus going away alone, even when people needed Him. He deliberately chose solitude. The more hectic our lives become, the more necessary is this quietness. When it is impossible to break away physically to a place of solitude for a day or so in order to think and pray over a hard decision, there is one thing which I think helps—do not speak about the decision to anyone but God for forty-eight hours at least. Just hold it before Him alone. Keep your mouth shut for two days. Pray. Listen. Seek his counsel.

Try this, too—sit before Him for fifteen consecutive minutes in silence, focusing your mind on the words of Psalm 86:11 (NEB), "Guide me, O Lord, that I may be true to thee and follow thy path."  □

## 30 Love of the World

JOHN TELLS US in his first letter that anyone who loves the world is a stranger to the Father's love. We are not to set our hearts on the world or anything in it. These words have been interpreted in many strange ways by different varieties of Christians, and I have puzzled much over them. The word used in the original is *cosmos*, which means the whole created order. Is there nothing here that I am allowed to love? What about the thundering, flashing sea that I see from my window? What about the rose on my desk, or even this house where I live with its warmth and pleasantness, the cup of tea in mid-afternoon, the books on my shelves? They are not going to last forever. If I love them, am I then a stranger to my heavenly Father's love?

It has helped me to think of John's words in this manner: To love the world in the wrong way is to love it without knowing the Father's love. It is when a man knows Him and receives everything *from his hand* that the world is redeemed for him, no longer a snare and in opposition to the love of God. We must love the world only through and because of the Father, not instead of. Our ultimate concern must be God Himself. He is eternal. His gifts are not always so.

Lord, may no gift of yours ever take your place in my heart. Help me to hold them lightly in an open palm, that the supreme object of my desire may always be You and You alone. Purify my heart—I want to love You purely. □

## 31 A Devious Repentance

RECENTLY I COMMITTED A SIN of what seemed to me unpardonable thoughtlessness. For days I wanted to kick myself around the block. What is the matter with me? I thought. How could I have acted so? "Fret not thyself because of evildoers" came to mind. In this case the evildoer was myself, and I was fretting. My fretting, I discovered, was a subtle kind of pride. "I'm really not that sort of person," I was saying. I did not want to be thought of as that sort of person. I was very sorry for what I had done, not primarily because I had failed someone I loved, but because my reputation would be smudged. When my reputation becomes my chief concern, my repentance has a hollow ring. No wonder

Satan is called the deceiver. He has a thousand tricks, and we fall for them.

Lord, I confess my sin of thoughtlessness and my sin of pride. I pray for a more loving and a purer heart, for Jesus' sake.   □

*The Elisabeth Elliot Newsletter* is published every other month and is sent to all who request it. Recent issues have contained articles on prayer, self-sacrifice, abortion, and raising children. Regular features include recommended reading, prayer requests, and news of tapes and books, as well as Elisabeth Elliot's travel schedule. For a sample copy write to:

**The Elisabeth Elliot Newsletter
P.O. Box 7711
Ann Arbor, Michigan 48107**